A Journeyman's Tales

Recollections in Verse

by

Bradley Garrett

A Journeyman's Tales

Recollections in Verse

by

Bradley Garrett

A Journeyman's Tales
Recollections in Verse

First published as "Teasury of a Life" in 2013 by
Koel Koel
New and extended edition published in 2022 by
Rack and Rune Publishing
rackandrune.com

All rights reserved. This book is copyright. Apart from any fair dealings for the purpose of private study, criticism, research or review as permitted under the Copyright Act (Australia), no part may be reproduced by any process without written permission.

© 2022 Bradley Garrett

ISBN: 978-0-6454362-4-2
Cataloguing-in-Publication entry is available from the National Library of Australia
https://catalogue.nla.gov.au/

Frontispiece: "For Keeps" by D'Arcy Doyle. Used with permission.
Thanks to Jennefer Doyle.

Photograph of Arthur Stace © Copyright HammondCare.
Used with permission. www.hammondcare.com.au.
Thanks to David Martin and Peter Hallett.

Illustrations by Fiona Tsang & Graham Davidson.
Editing, typesetting and layout by Michael Jameson & Graham Davidson.

Contents

Journeyman Sonnet	11
La Femme	12
Love	13
Father Apart	14
Save the First Dance for Me	15
Home	16
Lad of Nine	17
Threepences and Sixpences—1940s	18
Summer Swallows	19
1943	20
Gotta be Worth Two Bob	21
'Clothes Props! Clothes Props!'	23
Ode to the Horse and Cart: The Nose Knows	24
Cape York Cattle Dog—1946	25
Laisser-Aller	26
Everything Happens for a Reason	27
Eternity	29
Too Marvelous for Words	30
April 25	31
Hallowed Ground: WW2	32
Rat Gang, East Brisbane - Circa 1946	33
Ticketty-boo	34
Letitia: Nineteenth Century	35
My Pal Goldie	37
Matilda	38
Sunday Afternoon at Mowbray Park - Circa 1948	39

1951	40
At Dusk	41
60/40 Dance at the Town Hall - Circa 1951	43
The Hokey Pokey–1951	44
Journey's Harvest	45
1956-1958	46
Beyond the Pale	47
Cherubs	48
Waltzing Matilda	49
Seaview	50
Kindness	52
An Ode to all Composers of Music and Lyrics	53
Harmonica Virtuoso Lawrence Cecil Adler, 1914–2001	54
Liz Taylor 1932-2011	55
Demise of a Dancer	56
Cavill Avenue–1962	57
Huxley and the 'Doors' of Perception	58
Spring Foliage in the Antipodes	59
Strictly for the birds	60
Spring Foliage in the Antipodes	61
A Stormy Night One Summer	62
The Outhouse	63
Summer Fantasy	64
The Table of Knowledge	65
High Rollers: a sonnet	66
Mother Incarnate	68
Mother & Father	69
Touch The Heart	70
Now is All There is	71

Heaven on Earth	72
Spiritus Sancti	73
Bees	74
Sepia Moon	75
Wrens at Pepper Trees	76
Debeyers Hill	77
Country Train	78
Weekends Away	79
Wilderness Road at Lovedale	80
An Autumn Morn	81
Alpha and Omega	82
MSF	83
Yesterdays	85
Dare to Dream	86
Ode to a Gemini	87
Prime Years Waning	88
From the Coalface	89
Transition	90
Roadside Ballad	91
What do you make of it?	92
A Very Good Year	93
Classic Beauty	94
Wheelchairs and Prams	95
Early Morning – Bird Songs	96
HARDSHIPS	97
Individuals	98
Death's Door	99
Afternoon Seabreeze, Gold Coast, Oz	100
Moreton Bay—Sand Crabs—20th Century	101

Sixties Nouveau	102
Stress and Strain at the Pub	103
Falling Apart	104
Good Deed	105
Be Cause	106
Twilight	107
Hauteur	108
Truculence	109
Forgiveness	110
Leg Up	111
Life is Good	112
Quandary	113
Beware the Iceman	114
Utopia wanting	115
Ulmara	116
Esprit de Corps	117
Golf: 'Sword of Damocles'	118
Love Thy Neighbour	119
What Works!	120
Journey of Life	121
Home	122
At Dusk	123
Betwixt & Between	124
Colour of Autumn	125
"Fair Go" to "Have a Go"	126
All There Is	127
Bounce of the Ball	128
Boat People–1770	129
Formal Wear at the 'Kaffe'	130

Home Sweet Home—"Food on the Table"	131
Gold Coast—Main Beach	132
Anathema for the Dreamer?	133
Hunter Valley—Bird Watch	134
Elegiac Air Waves	135
Pokolbin Village—Broke Road	136
Opportunity	137
Maternal Light	139
Act on cue	140
Rapscallion	141
Over the Line	142
Regent Theatre—Brisbane	143
Liberté	144
A Spiritual Message	145
Semper Fidelis	146
Invitation to Lunch	147
Time	148
Summer Landscapes in Oz	149
Heaven For Me	150
Morning Malarkey	151
Today Is the Only Day We Have	152
Pavarotti Passing	153
Persuasion of Black	154
Oxymoron	155
Signs in the Solar System	156
Just 'Being'	157
'Orange Sky' Founder	158
Full Moon, at Large	159
Willy Wag Tail	160

Rainbow's End	161
Summer Madness	162
Everything Matters, Yet Nothing Matters	163
Mother Country England	164
Ace Tennis Pros	165
Camp Road Sentient	166
Victory in the Vines	167
St Catherine de Siena, 1347 - 1380	168
Who Are You?	169
Oakey Creek Road, Hunter Valley	170
Ebb Tide: Life Going Out	171
Channel de Beyers	172
Oz Ground Up	173
Greta, Hunter Valley	174
What's the Score? Imp to Limp	175
Gift of Life	176
West Wind: Terrible Day to Be Out In	177
Smell	178
Latitude 40 South	179
To Obtain Wisdom, Observe More	180
Wistful Winter Mornin'	181
Life	182
Eternity	183
Stillness	184
Puzzlement	185
Pacific Ocean Angst	186
Other Side of Humdrum	187
Nebuchadnezzar's Ashes Ascend	188
Oh Me, Oh My	189

Exit Winter, Enter Spring	190
Equity	191
True Blue D'Arcy Doyle	192
Moot Point	193
Energy and Light	194
Arlington Memorial in Step	195
Given the Opportunity	196
Karma-Loka: Verses 114	197
Top Knot - Crested Pigeon	198
New England	199
1940s Bread and Dripping	200
Grim Companions at Reaper's Door	201
Passage of Time	202
Sounds of Silence	203
Breath of Life	204
Seniors' Lunch	205
Midnight Unfolding	206
Senior Years	207
The Petition	208
Paradigm Down Under Perusal: Test Cricket	209
The New Oligarch: 2015	210
People Business: Dichotomy	211
Pretender to Paradise	212
Food on the Table	213
Leonard Cohen's Hallelujah:	214
Thought-Provoking	215
If Only	216
The Bumbler	217
Lucky	218

Sulphur Tablets, 1942	219
Ingenuity and Human Endeavors	220
EIIR	221
Prosaic Choices	222
Quid Pro Quo	223
1950's East Sydney: Sonnet	224
Pro Bono Bird Feeder	225
Medal Moments	226
Welfare, 1960: How Times Have Changed	227
Curtain Calls: Winston Churchill	228
Golf Lessons: Tell Someone Who Cares	229
Ellen	230
A Load of Rubbish	231
AD: 1941	232
H. V. Divine Cradle	233
Contemplative	234
Heaven For Me	235
Be Careful What You Wish For	236
Ghoulish Galahs	237
Sign of Summer	238
2000 AD	239
My Squat	240
Tranquillity	241
Acknowledgments	243

Journeyman Sonnet

A journey's man's life, a rolling stone with no moss
Found friends and old, are gathered into his fold.
The bitter and the sweet, some gains—some loss
Observation and wit, the essential tools in his kit
Iconoclast no, nor a sheep who goes with the flow
Eagle like though, soaring high above paths below
In uncluttered space, seldom felt in that other place.
Reasoning here holds sway, others' teachings fade away.
At journeys end, perhaps the ultimate goal achieved
Become the best possible persona you ever believed.
Leaving behind all the religious dogma ever chattered
The struggle pain, over nothing that ever really mattered
Universe in all its profound perfection, begs the question
Be the best you really want to be, that is the suggestion!

bg2012

La Femme

I cannot conceive of any wonderment at any given time:
A picture more beautiful than of woman in her life prime.
This maternal matriarch of the entire human race
Illuminates the earthly all of God's every given grace.

bg2011

Love

Life is to live is to love,
A gilded gift from above,
All earth's treasures seem to pale;
This pure pleasure is not for sale.

bg1981

Father Apart

Of all life's pleasures that I've had
(there have been many, I might add),
there is nothing that does compare
than to see my child, playing there.
Her presence fills me with delight,
her memory lights each lonely night.
Never was there such a love to miss,
oh! how I hunger for her goodnight kiss.
Alchemy and loveliness in her adopted poses,
more enchanting than a garden of roses.
Her eyes are bright, her sighs are tender,
I'm so glad she's of the feminine gender.

bg1982
Dedicated to Georgina

Save the First Dance for Me

An imposing verandah railed open, from north through to west;
The stilted Queenslander caught the summer breeze best.
A broad handsome stairway reached up to a light lattice door,
Feigning security, for the delicately decked, vast wooden floor.

Through a languorous lobby, its frieze ceiling fifteen feet tall,
A mosaic leadlight, pasted patches of colour, to the alcove wall,
Mother's Steinway piano proclaimed promises of good and right,
Standing proudly on polished timbers, indeed, an inviting sight.
'Twas in this setting harmonious, a young mother and young son
Stumbled and steered through a waltz, his first lesson had begun.

bg2010

Home

Retreat is the home where one rests the feet
To drop one's guard away from people you meet
Eager years of enthusiasm to get it just right
Give added pleasure when you come home at night
The harmony of nature is right there to behold
Nesting birds in the trees that live to grow old
Bees are so busy hopping from flower to flower
Then to complete the cycle down comes a shower
The stirring of a breeze seems to rustle the trees
Then leaves waft down as gentle as you please
They land on the wet ground and lay there to rot
No longer hot, the flowers and shrubs perk up a lot
Magpies and kookaburras contesting the space
Draw the contest and retire with grace
Lizards that are frilled and lizards that are not
Roam the lawns and gardens and eat grubs a lot
It's all so natural and relaxing to see
I can think of no other place I'd rather be
Barking dogs can sometimes dismantle the peace
The interruption is minor for soon it will cease.

bg1980

Lad of Nine

The ice hooks could grapple two blocks at a time,
quite a load for a lad of nine.
3am start at Woolloongabba ice works;
boys sought these scarce paid lurks.
Though two blocks in both hands were 14lb each,
a full load was just in reach.
Nine hours of filling numerous ice chests
was one of the week's hardest tests.
For Queensland houses built on stilts,
traipsing up long stairways induced body wilts.
Soon enough we've finished the job,
totally buggered, but made me five bob.

bg2009

Threepences and Sixpences–1940s

A Christmas pudding, dome shaped and steaming
Rich Brandy sauce awash, glistening and gleaming
The ritual climax to the annual Festive day feast
New Year resolutions to resolve resultant obese
Young children devoid of such querulous qualms
Though sated scouring the pud, for it's hidden alms
Part of Gran's wily plan to entertain at the dinner
Implanting zac and tray bits that are so much thinner.

bg2012

Summer Swallows

A fiery heat had arrived by nine,
the sky was blue, the day was fine.
And as I lay in summer's wake,
something roused me, enticed a step to take.
What was that vague yet familiar sound,
that made me step out to look around?
Behold! Criss-cross hues of blues and browns,
an army of swallows acting like clowns.
Chirping shrilly, as they dived in a way,
as if to proclaim it will be soon Christmas day.
Amazing, they arrive the same time each year,
to display their boldness and lend good cheer!
Sparrows and doves sweltering in the shade,
pretend not to notice the little wings flayed.
Of swooping swallows in a desperate race,
who have arrived here to nest from a distant place.
To carry out nature's way unmolested,
and complete life's cycle uncontested.

bg1981

1943

At the time of my first communion in '43
The war had gone badly, badly as can be.
Millions of Soviet citizens had been killed
All Europe fallen, only Heil Hitler thrilled.

General Macarthur, his legions of troops, GIs
Camped in East Brisbane under balmy blue skies.
Air raid sirens screamed each afternoon at three
Intimidating this island of peace and tranquility.

GIs at night came out to play, come what may,
Chanced upon our residence, from the fence
Sighted a 22 year old woman blond and buxom
Daughter of Aunty Jesse, a visiting Sydney cousin.

One succeeded this blond to meet, and then treat
Short scarce items to eat, plus candy and pretzels,
Americans had no such shortages, unlike our selves
Never before seen, these foreign items on shelves.

Blokes became guys, girls became gals
Homesick GIs became our new-found pals,
Nothing but peril, their fate was in store
As these troops soon bound for Phillipines shore.

The Japanese were expecting Macarthur's return
Indeed to their peril as many in hell would burn
Though now long gone, I oft remember the union
The flavour of pretzels and my first communion.

bg2010

Gotta be Worth Two Bob

From L/s/d ninepence halfpenny up to a shilling
1941-2. Prices for 'sheet music' the likely billing
Lunchtime in Penny's, Brisbane Queen Street
City dwellers thronged, would gather to meet
To hear the latest tunes was a welcome treat
A piano playing young mother would also sing
Cheers and claps, to some eyes tears could bring
World at war meant worry sickness and despair
The young son viewing his mother in the chair
Playing and singing, for a time without a care.
He loved her dearly for helping, just being there

bg2013
Dedicated to Melodie.

'Clothes Props! Clothes Props!'

A crumpled cart man brought his cart horse to a stop,
Fumbled for his fine cut, bought at the corner shop.
A wispy thin cigarette paper found its way to his lips,
Between grinding palms now, aromatic aroma trips.
The cart man cursed as dry lips locked the paper fast,
Fixed by a lick, the ritual rolling finally began at last.
The durry alight and smoking, a sanguine sight it proved,
Embouchure permitted 'Gee up!' and the old cart horse moved.
River stones aside the gutter did scrunch and splatter,
Wash-day was a family matter, lots of work and chatter.
Time to bellow clothes props: 'Clothes Props! Clothes Props!'
Just in case you need one, the courtly cart man stops.

bg2011

Ode to the Horse and Cart: The Nose Knows

A clip clopping Clydesdale with a white blaze on her head,
17 hands, quiet and content, her nose bag keeps her well fed,
Blinkered she follows the bread mans' deliveries, not led,
The light load she is pulling, steaming hot, fresh baked bread,
No bell ringing rouser needed, whiffs of wafting aromas instead,
Eve had her apple in Eden, thank heavens for our daily bread.

bg2010

Cape York Cattle Dog—1946

When I was a boy, just after the war
Eldest brother locked his bedroom door
Steam trained to a Coen cattle station
Land most inhospitable in the nation
Adventure to work at something new
Trying his teen hand, a tyro jackeroo
In heartland of indigenous black fella
Tribal striped with red white and yella
Working as mates offered much to gain
From master managers of fragile terrain
Soon two years flew by, time to go home
With some evidence of his daring roam
leather whip to wield an explosive crack
Nulla nulla clubs for defence and attack
Plus a blue heeler pup just off the teat
Ultimate treasure for a young boy's treat

bg2012

Laisser-Aller

Sunday dinner sharp at noon, the air was still and stinking hot,
A sit down hot dinner: Mum, Dad, Gran and siblings four, the lot.
A tall man thinner appeared, knocked and stared from the door,
Looking pale and drained, explained, he just returned from the war.
Stating his case, he was looking for work, indeed for any odd chore,
Unashamedly saying that he was in need of a meal—nothing more!
Assuage did prevail, with war far behind him, no longer to assail;
To this day I am so very moved to share this true enduring tale.

bg2009

Everything Happens for a Reason
- *A Universal Truth* -

See the good plus see the bad,
see all the times you've ever had
The sum total being the measure
of life's accumulated treasure
Some folk on bad luck do dwell,
but there's another side as well
Universal wisdom tells us all,
no bad luck means no luck at all.
If you've not experienced cold,
how do you know warm, we are told.
So buckle up and enjoy the ride,
take what's dealt you in your stride.
You may but once come this way,
make the most of every day.

bg2009

A rare photograph of Arthur Stace (seated) at Chippendale Hotel. © Copyright HammondCare. Used with permission.

Eternity

The one line gospel of Arthur Malcolm Stace,
Blessed by a Supreme Sovereign's grace.
Writing from a Calligrapher's hand one guessed,
Surely not from a derelict's arm, stressed.
No fine garments to be seen, nor altars of gold
To preach from, to reach out to his fold.
Neither a fire nor brimstone sermon,
Simply, a path or wall to write on.
As seen in many a Sydney city street,
The unseen Stace at night on his beat.
'Eternity' just one mighty word of impact,
That keeps the mind alert and intact!

bg2010

Too Marvelous for Words

A penny ride in a tram trolley
Accompanied by just an ice-cream and lolly
Was Saturday arvo at the flicks
Hopping along with Cassidy, Tarzan, or Tom Mix.
Splurging that hard earned weekly bob
Pushing that lawn hand-mowing job.
After viewing the serial, we've made merry
With comic Tom and Jerry.
Then for last followed the main feature,
Be it Lassie, or a King Kong creature.
Back home serial radio was king,
Or around the piano family gathered to sing.
Those pre teen time years, halcyon,
Too marvelous for words, bygone.

bg2009

April 25

One hand-held sign seen at kerbside each year
Embodies the thoughts for all, gathered to cheer,
Braids emotions of men marching in neat ranks.
This metaphoric message is a single word, 'Thanks'.
Folk roar with approval when old vets march by,
Pageantry and memory flood, cause many to cry,
For our sons sent to distant shores certain to die.
Let this Anzac Spirit calibrate each generation,
As we commemorate each year with this celebration,
Pray its fierce furnace can forge a great nation.

bg2009

Hallowed Ground: WW2
Gallant camaraderie we honour them yet

This was the land the Japanese over ran and kept.
The very same, where Weary Dunlop dwelt and slept
Where mates, war warriors, worked worried and wept
Sentenced to a dire death of desperate deprivation
Seemingly unaided by prayers, and the pleas of a nation
Freedom denied by the Emperor, and Polemarch inept.

bg2012

Rat Gang, East Brisbane - Circa 1946

Stodgy looking characters in britches and braces,
Hard living lines etched into leather-tanned faces,
Searching for rat holes under houses and ditches,
Armed with an arsenal of fox terrier bitches.

Ground level aviary looked the place to start,
A ready-made mess hall, for rodent repast,
Brass-nozzled hose end, thrust into the shaft,
Followed the terrain from opening to aft,
When obstructed and could proceed no more,
Water tap turned on and opened full bore,
Terriers pawing and prancing in anticipation,
Denying escape routes, and emancipation.

bg2011

Ticketty-boo

If one should ever say hello, no matter who,
In the customary manner, with 'How do you do?'
Cause it is really seldom I'm ever feeling blue
Cordially shall I respond 'I'm really ticketty-boo.'
Hard to imagine otherwise in this great estate,
Australia is my homeland, it really is first rate,
Where everyone you meet turns out to be a mate
Hard to imagine otherwise in this great estate.

bg2009

Letitia: Nineteenth Century

My Grandma looked ancient through my first seven years
Her voice cracked and quavered, eyes streamed with tears
Nineteenth-century harshness not reflected in her kindly face
Belying the perilous journey of another time and place
Two of her seven babies died, in process of giving birth
Setbacks aplenty - yet her humble home draped in mirth
Harsh times, modern antibiotic medicines yet to discover
Early twentieth-century mothers, faced jeopardy to recover
No TV, washing machines, refrigerators, or electric stoves
No wonder those ANZAC-boy bunch were such tough coves.

bg2015

My Pal Goldie

The new owner so polite,
though he'd never take charge any day or night.
Goldie had landed a great provider,
but he could never be a capable rider.
An accomplished rider has a very good seat,
light reins, a bit that's sweet.
The untrained rider the horse can tell,
a likely spill if not balanced well.
Goldie a racehorse through and through,
galloping was all he ever knew.
The flashy chestnut now past his prime,
eagerly longed his retirement time.
Handlers never held trophies or celebration cakes,
only post race day wakes.
Punters and horses share the pain,
winning is the only name of the game.

Legendary punter, Hollywood George Bedser, was on the right tack.
Famously said: 'More heartaches than hoofbeats found
on a racetrack'
The knackery looked a likely wager, but for the timely turn
of a stranger.

bg2009

Matilda

A swaggy's backpack is his mate, his Matilda in a sling
As he wanders freely, like the bird on the wing
Savouring the stillness of pure air he has his fill
That conjures up alacrity, to forge a steely will
Needed for the deepest creek and the highest hill.
When the sun sinks, when the day is done at last
Time to unpack Matilda, fire up the billy tea fast
Break out the victuals for a camp oven repast
Then as before, repack Matilda after breakfast.

bg2011

Sunday Afternoon at Mowbray Park - Circa 1948

Spawning perch choked the Brisbane River far and wide.
Truant boys precariously perched on retaining wall rocks,
Shoeless in shorts, disheveled, with unruly forelocks.
Cheese/dough bait cast float line, against wind and tide,
Bouncing and bobbing, enticing fish to bite or to hide.

Musicians reaching the Rotunda, erect sheet music stands,
Mowbray uniforms, all spit and polish, like regular brass bands.
Some strolling local families browsing, just looking around,
Begin surrounding the Rotunda, then seated upon the ground.
Anxiously now, the conductor chafing, raps the baton aloud,
To a man they begin, as melodic brass captivates the crowd.

bg2011

1951

Saturday night atop the hill at Ascot—
        Cloudland ballroom was the spot.
Where half of young Brisbane danced,
        chanced a meet, to give it a shot,
With Billo Smith and his band of renown,
        top swing band in Brisbane town.
Proudly presented medleys of Quickstep,
        Foxtrot, Pride of Erin, to trot.
Eagerly awaited was Woody Herman's Golden Wedding,
        on cue milieu,
Where prescience precluded hope,
        of Billo ever hitting that elusive top note.
Stylish crewcuts, stove pipe trousers,
        a thin white belt, jiving at full pelt,
Frowned upon, in a far removed section,
        behind a cordoned thick rope.
Harbinger that the classic ballroom dancing
        was fading, without hope.
After the exhilaration and exertion, when sweat dried,
        all tension died,
Softly, softly played 'Besame Mucho'
        time for up close and smoocha.
The refrain: 'Love me forever and make
        all my dreams come true'.
When Saturday night arrived—
        there's nothing else you would rather do.

bg2010

At Dusk

Shrill bird sounds penetrate the dusk,
to pierce eardrums like a rapier's thrust.
Flocks of birds descend from flight,
as they prepare to roost the night.
What ensues is an unholy fight,
as each one jostles for the space that's right.
The row-de-dow is heard each evening,
leaving aching eardrums sorely grieving.

bg2009

60/40 Dance at the Town Hall - Circa 1951

Flight to a Friday night dance, at South Brisbane Town Hall.
Inside a bevy of beauties wait seated, beside the hallway wall.

    Enthusiastic glowing faces,
    impatient to commence their paces.
    Daring to dream, pray for romance,
    'Would you like to dance?'

Budding bosoms struggle to fit, in Mum's hand-me-down dress,
secure in knowing, Helena Rubenstein covers puberty's mess.
Boys' bravado drumming up courage, slide to a nervous walk,
disguising a carefully planned position to pounce and to talk.

    Sometimes a walk needs be a scurry,
    lest beaten by those in a hurry.
    In an instant all the girls can be taken,
    unless you are sadly mistaken.
    Maybe there are two sitting it out;
    rejection—'Sorry!'—turn about
    with eyes downcast, reddened face,
    crestfallen and needing space.
    A pass out needed to rethink,
    haul oneself back from the brink.
    Youthful vigours soon recharge,
    ego elevated, to slick and at large.
    Lesson heeded that very day,
    then it's full charge, back to the fray.

bg2011

The Hokey Pokey–1951

Ma Sommerville's Guest House
the spot to bunk the night
Greenmount Beach not far
but just out of sight
Be it a young bloke or lad
A woman or girl bikini clad
hokey pokey was all the rage
enacted upon a golden stage
first taste of freedom to be had
abandoned ethics of mum and dad.

bg2011

Journey's Harvest

1930's-early 40's, a hangover, post Queen Victoria's blend
Horses outnumbered cars, clothes we did make and mend.
For some, Tom Sawyer, Twain's adventure driven world, wild
Feverishly embracing daylight, as gallivanting barefoot child
Cycle to school traffic, trams and hills, no fear for these foe.

National Service call up chimes untimely end to teen clock
En route to Sydney Woolloomooloo, Garden Island dry dock
Awaits a floating 720 ft grey predator to board, get to know
800 sailors lined the flight deck, the ship's brass band blow
Nostrils flare in stiff sea breeze, exhilaration shines on show.

Fiji turned out en masse to welcome a first visit in ten years
Lined up, the ship's crew and band were drowned in cheers
1955, Fiji a la natural, drank root Kava not imported beers
Followed days of merriment, back slapping of Aussie peers
Leaving harbour stinging strains of 'Isa Lei' brought many tears.

bg2013

1956-1958

Dead bodies floating by ship's side—
some humour—but no one cried.
Chinese painters of Australian ships—
matter of fact—no pursed lips.
Little, if any, value for Humanity,
the very antithesis of Christianity.
Knife cutting air, strange sounds,
a distant culture curiously abounds.

Further north, Korea, in backward stages,
women at riverside of all ages.
Hordes, stone pummeling their washing,
for themselves or for wages.
Yoked oxen with a V-shaped sleigh,
ferrying loads throughout the day.
Square proportions of body and face,
characteristics of the Korean race.
Time stood still in its war-ravaged land,
buildings barely able to stand.
Japan enforced visitors' hygiene,
discard shoes at door, or create a scene.
Courtesy and manners were five star,
extended to noisy patrons in bar.
Endless duties in readiness trained,
excitement dulled and senses drained.
Summers and winters quickly came,
left as quickly as an extinguished flame.
An overseas adventure leaving one spent,
time to sail south to the great continent.

bg2010

Beyond the Pale

Lord is there likely another war,
with more pain, death and grief galore?
Is the Book of Apocalypse now to be read,
countless millions to be dead?
Is the wealthy west so greedy,
where other life is deprivation and needy?
Please lead us to Eden once more,
away from misery, the blood, the gore.
Where altruism can prevail,
to leave discord, mayhem, beyond the pale.

bg2009

Cherubs

Behind those arcane portals at heaven's gate,
Lays a crèche of seraphic cherubs content to wait,
To fulfil an earthly brief, in a world filled with hate,
The Universe's gift to an expectant mother's girth,
Changing life's priorities, add meaning to life worth,
And bring great happiness and love to all at birth.

bg2009

Waltzing Matilda

Miss McPherson's tune had a rousing beat,
Patterson's words added an absolute treat.
Banjo Patterson traveled Queensland in 1895
It was there in Winton when he did arrive
That he hatched a notion that would forever survive.
For at Dagworth Station lived a Miss McPherson
Her composing well known, as she played in person.
She had played her new tune for all at the meet
So happy her work was deemed such a treat.
Banjo at this party being known for his wit
For amusement he claimed, he could put words to it.
Well, the rest is history, as they say,
Waltzing Matilda is here to stay,
well, at least in Oz, forever and a day.

bg2009

Seaview

There is something about being at sea,
especially the peace and freedom it gives me.
Crashing through barriers of wind and waves,
secure from the intrusions of vacuous raves.
What other occasion compares with the grace,
the luxury, the exuberance of so much space?
Where else can a rainbow appear so bright?
And oh! so close the moon and stars at night.
Inquisitive dolphins come to show the way,
at the bow of the ship, by night and by day.
They arrive in great numbers to race and to play,
so endearing are they, you wish they could stay.

Where else can a man spend so much time,
dreaming his dreams beyond the horizontal line?
Where else can a man enjoy so much cohesion,
removed from world plights and television?
Where else does the air so flatter the senses?
You can add to that: no traffic, no fences.
Food in abundance lies beneath the keel,
indeed, more than enough to get a good meal.
The gulls and the seabirds are another delight,
strong and willing, they rarely take fright.
A surfacing turtle now and then you'll find,
they don't stay long, they know man's unkind.
Gold and black sea snakes sometimes emerge,
it's a shame serpents are such a terrible scourge.

Then there's the thrill after sailing so long,
to arrive at some place and nothing's gone wrong.
Because danger prevails like some lurking spectre,
God fearing men pray it's no interceptor.
Even knowing all that, I'll continue to roam,
for the sea to me is like being at home.

bg1982

Kindness

No need to be tricky or smart, kindness is straight from the heart.
Every kind loving act will enrich and reward like no other art
In its giving or receiving, surely the freeway to 'God Bless'.
If practiced, we together could reduce duress and world stress.
Who amongst us could forget Mandela's struggle of 67 years?
How he overcame adversity, injustices and apartheid fears?
When finally to be released from prison, broken and brittle,
Yet for all his suffering—bitterness, revenge——he showed little.
As seen in his saintly face, a template for the whole human race,
A beacon of love and kindness, shining on us all to embrace.

bg2009

An Ode to all Composers of Music and Lyrics

Songs we know and adore leave us begging for more.
Souls retain their lingering strain of a sweet refrain amour.
Slow, slow, quick quick slow, allow the feelings to flow,
While wanton feet, tap to the beat, of the cadenced tempo.
Try to imagine a crime, life without music and lyrics that rhyme.
These eerily mark so fine, tragedy, triumph, events in our time.
A metronomed almanac of life's years, as recorded through the ears,
May guide heartstrings so dear, to past sorrows, romance and cheer,
Or elevate our emotional ascension, to a heavenly, higher dimension.

Pray Lord, see fit to maintain these stations for future generations.
So, composers and authors, salutations! A tribute from all nations,
For your entertainment lauded, the amour you've afforded.
You are truly loved, allegorically acclaimed, and applauded.

bg2009

Bradley Garrett

Harmonica Virtuoso Lawrence Cecil Adler, 1914–2001

A concierge glared a disapproving look
as I approached a cross-legged figure in a foyer nook.
A refracted light from a glazed window space
shone down on this well known worldly face.
Savoring his seldom solitary state, his 87 years heavy,
longevity has its price, its levy.

Risking reproach, without hesitation and with no notification,
I began to address this man.
This legendary virtuoso Larry Adler, Lawrence Cecil Adler and
me, one of a legion, called fan.
A Dorothy Dixer about his career,
music theatre, the arts, he matter-of-factly began to tier:
Greta Garbo and Chaplin, from Rachmaninoff to Ravel,
just some of many stories he could tell.
Then Einstein, Gershwin, Crosby and Astaire,
all friends through life he had known so well

Chancing further discussion, still eager to discover,
I inquired about home, his family, his mother.
The old man excited got to his feet,
for soon he explained he'd be back home, his daughter to greet.
It's ironic in his world choked with triumph, but no mystery,
Larry's home and family, the lasting life victory.

bg2009

Liz Taylor 1932-2011

A siren of old tinsel town, who once wore the crown,
The envy of every other actor, and woman in every town.
Her pleading starry violet eyes, every mortal man beguiles,
Replete flawless figure, staging couturiers' latest styles.
Quo ad the frail voice tremor, that weakens one's knees,
Every look, every sigh, every smile, did naught but please.
In an alter space, to be sure, you be still divining,
In some angelic place, with velvet hair still shining.

bg2011

Demise of a Dancer

Ah yes, about fame, now, what was her name, sublime?
The movie was simply divine, surely you remember the time?
Dancing with Fred, all in red, with jet-black slicked back hair,
Her agile limbs were dynamite, as they swayed in step with Astaire.
Effortlessly the master strutted, strolled and danced to the beat,
While she pursued him with passion, her ballerina's lithe, nimble feet.
Ah yes, it's coming to me now, I remember too, smiling lips so red
The vision so clear, so lovely, yet her name eluding my head.
Dear, dear Cyd Charisse has passed on, aged four score and six.
Always, I'll fondly remember her, on that big silver screen at the flicks.

bg2008

Cavill Avenue–1962

Mutton bird oil dispensed by the pith helmet man
Applied by a blast spray ensured an all over tan
After surf and sand, lunch with Stan Bourne's band
Food and vaudeville in Cavill's beer garden land
Across the road at Digby's 'Blue Room' stake
Scantily clad go-go girls shimmy and shake
Upstairs first floor, at the open window space
Old folk stare up with disgust, a look of distaste
The young bloods clamour to be on the pace
Gather at 'the Bird Watchers Bar', Cavill's corner
Glass facade to note each female performer
To greet and meet at a favourite drinking well
Bragging boys bravado, lots of kiss and tell
Refreshments repast, a nap, get ready for a date
At the Beachcomber, with the girls and your mate.

Huxley and the 'Doors' of Perception

Experimenting to find a new form of glee
Aldous Huxley entered a world containing LSD
Accounting of doors to delusion and deception
Mind bending convention and normal perception
Helping Jim Morrison to get higher and higher
On stage with bourbon, Jim's condition became dire
His doors of perception began rapidly eroding
After just 25 years, his mind finally exploding.

bg2009

Spring Foliage in the Antipodes

Awakening spring detected by new shades of colour green;
New sprigs in trees alone count for at least seventeen.

> Banksia's patent pastel thrills,
> against a mass of red bottlebrush twills.
> Here, lorikeets feast and seem to hold sway,
> chattering aloud in their bird talk way.
> Skeletal trees have no showing,
> dead or alive? No way of knowing.

They embrace the landscape looking weary, and wallowing,
Yet bolstered by hope, with sucker growth following.
Mighty maples shrouded with russet clusters, that fairly adorn,
Soon tire and tumble, to impose its colour carpet on the lawn.

> Dormant vines eager to budburst,
> renew, and absolve winters worst.
> Prickly rosebushes trailed to a trellis,
> climbing skyward, without threat or malice.
> Offering incense to the gods above
> in gratitude for life, with thanks and love.
> All these things nature brings,
> with changing season, each chapter sings.
> Breathtaking beauty that chimes,
> beautiful beholdings to our minds.

bg2009-11

Strictly for the birds

Winded from waving, old palm leaves droop and drop,
Leaving a circular ladder formed, from near the top,
Here, a thicket of thatched ferns enters into wedlock,
Positioned perfectly, for finches and lorikeets to flock.
Many more persuasions of birdlife too can be found,
In this private secure site, safe, and high above ground.
Groaning green palms laden with fruit, in reach to nourish,
A purveyor providing larder, for its village to flourish.

bg2011

Spring Foliage in the Antipodes

Awakening spring detected by new shades of colour green;
New sprigs in trees alone count for at least seventeen.

    Banksia's patent pastel thrills,
    against a mass of red bottlebrush twills.
    Here, lorikeets feast and seem to hold sway,
    chattering aloud in their bird talk way.
    Skeletal trees have no showing,
    dead or alive? No way of knowing.

They embrace the landscape looking weary, and wallowing,
Yet bolstered by hope, with sucker growth following.
Mighty maples shrouded with russet clusters, that fairly adorn,
Soon tire and tumble, to impose its colour carpet on the lawn.

    Dormant vines eager to budburst,
    renew, and absolve winters worst.
    Prickly rosebushes trailed to a trellis,
    climbing skyward, without threat or malice.
    Offering incense to the gods above
    in gratitude for life, with thanks and love.
    All these things nature brings,
    with changing season, each chapter sings.
    Breathtaking beauty that chimes,
    beautiful beholdings to our minds.

bg2009-11

A Stormy Night One Summer

A lightning flash x-rays the trees,
and lights the night before it flees.
Like a scene from Hansel-Gretel tale,
as Heavens rant and Heavens rail
Crickets creaking tones afar do fly,
to be in concert with those nearby
Loudly proclaim their presence,
cloaking night noir with an eerie essence
Then hail and tempest of the summer storm
add cool comfort to the warm
From a firmament in high heaven sent,
soon, its fearful ferocity spent
Then follows a defiant stillness, rest,
at the departing intruder's behest.
Deafening silence in complete contrast,
inverse equal to what has passed
Senses paralysed in the electrified space,
soon return with normal grace.
Gradually, movement in the night,
breaks the spell of storm cast smite.
Vaulted in the sky dwells a Talisman,
universally playing out His plan
Signs off on this portfolio feature,
for the good of man and every creature
Though power is cut, there is no light,
peace may be found on such a night
Let the tempest strike pervade land's heart,
and rejuvenate a brand new start.

bg2009

The Outhouse

1972 was a stellar year for Qld's Brisbane city
Surveyor Clem Jones newly elected Lord Mayor
Applauded and elected for his skills and flair
Few suburbs had WCs, which was such a pity
This condition gave rise to countless a ditty
Great progress made, with vigour and verve
Only Clem showed the nettle and the nerve
WC Crapp porcelain within the first year
Leather padded cartman, about to disappear
As Lord Mayor, Clem would have no peer.

bg2011

Summer Fantasy

A high summer horizon moon spawned a silky, silvery glow
Over land and sea and all that inhabited the earth below
Ghost Head Nebula, too, chimed in from the Milky Way
To add stark startling brightness, that turned night into day
Confused oceans and rivers occasioned new watermarks high
Low-lying properties inundated, with no access, no passers by
Whim, chicanery, cunningly contrived by way of heaven's sky?
Or was this all a fantasy, as seen by a bewitched besotted eye.

bg2010

The Table of Knowledge

When the night has fled, and bid its final adieu,
And the ground is wet, and still covered with dew,
Marks the time when wise men get together,
At coffee shops and eateries, on Avenue Tedder.
Outside sits Keith, full of intent,
now that senior Keith's in retirement.
Roly-poly Max is at the scene,
he has his smile on the usual highbeam.
Then there's Ron, Blair, Jack and Bernie,
bruised, but not bettered, by life's long journey.
How long they do chatter,
solving all that's the matter.
Listen! Hear what they say,
bet you—it's a better way.
Three score years, plus ten or more,
be these weathered men of folklore.
If advice you seek from these men of good heart,
they may be willing to impart:
A way through the maze of life's byways and paths,
Lest wrong turns afford you aftermaths.
Much may be learned from this hand callused college
Should good fortune one day find you seated at this

bg2009

High Rollers: a sonnet

Fwd porthole met mooring pylon with a mighty bash
A pitch black night, just metres to sight, invites a crash
14 hours steaming, fishing Cape Moreton and beyond
Hauling in hungry sea bream in the shallows, ebb tide
Post full day catching mackerel, lures running each side
Rolling sea, sun and work, can down a sailor to his knees
4x Gold stubbies, esky iced down, be the antidote to appease.
Behind Glass House Mountains the sun has sunk so fast
Time to square away and end, to punch back home at last
Rev up to the shallow water cutting, as it's becoming dark
Sth East whipped up swells, hard to make out the mark.
Narrow nautical miles of cutting lights, blurring into sight
Radar turned on, and tuned to navigate through the night
Finally the Port of Brisbane, came to ships abeam a port
God, another two hours sailing beginning to feel like mort.

bg2013

Dedicated to the late, great Keith Williams - Sea World, Hamilton Island etc - as a tribute to him and his peers. You Main Beach men of enterprise and vision, you have been a great source of inspiration for me over a lifetime. By your deeds, I've been encouraged to have a go, to punch above my weight.

Mother Incarnate

A thousand faces walk on by
They neither distract, turn head nor eye
The tall the short, the in between
That special one, yet to be seen
At last, behold, a shrouded face
Unmarked and pure with God's shining grace,
Why has she appeared to the human race?
This astral Nymph from her heavenly place.

bg1984

Mother & Father

Mother and father are still alive
Approaching the age of four score and five,
One has religion, the other has not.
In some ways they wish for what the other has got.

bg1984

Touch The Heart

Occasions evoking chest-churning emotions
Enabling, disabling potent alchemy potions
Tense tight chest muscles strained and stressed
Partially eased by gasped air expressed.

Like when you left the tot alone, at the school gate
The child's very first day, left in a trembling state

Or lowering your mum into her last resting place
Finally at peace with the entire human race.

When seeing Jessica sail through the heads
After 7 months in harness, her legs just like lead

Did your eyes well with tears, or just seem
When Susan first sang 'I Dreamed a Dream'?

We are all different—that you can tell—but our
Emotions are drawn from the very same well.

bg2010

Now is All There is

My being has cast but a small shadow in this place
This place called Earth in timeless Universal Space
As I view my life through an arcane portal, showing
No east nor west, no before or after, only, all knowing.
A single template of all life lead, living and the dead
A capsule in cinemascope, where every life can be read.

bg2011

Heaven on Earth

Heaven is all about thee, for he who has eyes to see
Starry starry night, or sunny blue blue skies above
The purity and peace that is the white white dove
Every shrub, flower, creature, the wonder of each tree
Remove eye's blinkers, life's book soon enough be read
Enjoy, experience what you have, for soon enough be dead.

bg2011

Spiritus Sancti

When your 'ready sign' is showing, the Master will be near.
Be sure in the Absolute, knowing an Almighty truth is clear.
The Universe's source of healing will allay your every fear,
And be the protective hand over all that you hold dear.

bg2008

Bees

Consider the life of a bee...
Who forever works merrily...
Humming from flower to tree,
What a buzz ... being a bee.

bg2008

Sepia Moon

Oh! magic moon, you light the night,
unlike the Sun you counterfeit bright
We've accustomed to knowing you as a silvery fellow,
but tonight, tonight you're a sepia yellow!
At first glance you seem so oddly obscure,
behind tree tops, and houses, secure.
Then suddenly you appear at a break,
low on the horizon, and on the make.
Much more sculptured the lines of your face,
normally hidden in your usual high place.
Are you concocting a very high tide,
or is it a romance, or even a bride?
You appear so friendly, yet lonely up there,
no stars can I see where ever I stare.
Had you a reason to sweep them away,
or has your beauty cancelled their play?
Your appearance is seldom in any one year,
the stars, of course, have each night to appear.
They play second fiddle to your magic wand,
that vast orchestra, in the great beyond.

bg1982

Wrens at Pepper Trees

Amidst the manicured lawns and hedges green, at Pepper Trees
A legion of wiggling wren pogo-hopped and sang as if to please
Capped cobalt blue, plus face and vest, the proudly toted male rig
An oxymoron, a tiny body, with vertical paddle stick tail, twice as big.

bg2011

Debeyers Hill

Facing north atop a Pokolbin hill,
air so sweet and view to thrill
Rangey Brokenback to the west,
looking at its alluring best
Drought and fire did afflict,
but absolution granted, after conflict,
Escarpment gaps disappeared,
as new growth forward speared.
My goodness, Barrington Tops to due north
beg all to sally forth.
Even doffs its small ice cap,
and defers ingress without a trap.
Seaboard Newcastle flat to east,
shares a horde of breeze's feast
Audrey's vines the hill invade,
with army precision they do cascade.

bg2010

Country Train

Rushing late for a train can be traumatic,
Especially when closing doors are automatic.
If only ticket dispensers could be hurried,
The boarder would not be near so worried.
Country train travelers won't be relegated,
Ignoring the rules and signs, as regulated.
Like leaving luggage on an unticketed seat,
While some poor blighter stays on his feet.
After so many stops, numbers begin to swell,
As do other issues to tell, like noise and smell.
Foreign folk of many cultures on this train,
Appear to treat each other with distant disdain.
One might puzzle if altruism is just a word,
As that notion becomes oblique, even blurred.
From the window, note the bushland grandeur,
The affable antidote to restore mind's candour.

bg2009

Weekends Away

Wine Country welcomes city folks,
including the bold blokey blokes
When seen on arrival some appear to falter,
just like a fish that's out of water
Could it be the stillness, silence,
so far removed from city sounds and violence
Of chaotic choking traffic scenes,
with arguing men and women's screams
Given the passage of a day or two,
bouncy and buoyed by racy rendezvous
Tension and tautness seem to abate,
even though they still stay up late
Departing with a blaring horn telling,
the city bloke's way of fare-welling
Shattering every peace of the night,
startling wildlife, causing birds to take flight,
It's great they enjoy the weekend,
then leave a week for the country to mend.

bg2010

Wilderness Road at Lovedale

A rusty pall of dust, its worn washboard road is laid to rest
Newly laid gravel and tar, modern, to meet every day's test
Heavy duty machinery's groaning bellows, a barking-like sound
Intimidated wild-life abandons habitat, and nowhere to be found
Towering Caruarina trees bravely banded, united in a bold stand
Graciously grant light a passage, to filter inhibited to land
Provide a harbour for magpies, stoically guarding spring's new nest
Rosellas in racy colours, noisy mynah birds in numbers, have fled
Their waning timid hearts, found wanting when put to the test
Talga road nearby, already tamed, agreeable shelter for them instead.

bg2011

An Autumn Morn

Cottage windows wide open in a Lovedale estate,
As I luxuriate, comfy and warm, sleeping in late,
Cool country air washes over my prone body state.
Surfing the flow, a symphony of bird songs shrill,
From deep in the valley to atop of the hill.

bg2011

Alpha and Omega

The Alpha and Omega train will never be crowded or late,
For you to return to the universe with which you have a date.
You will shed all earthly feelings to make way for 'here and now'.
Remember, 'The All There Is' is waiting for you, the child apart.
To return home, rejoicing in her pure and loving heart.

bg2000

MSF

Thank you dear Lord for mankind with vocations
Medecins Sans Frontières is found in locations
treating disease and afflictions for one and for all
leaving loved ones and home, to answer the call.
Hail to them who sweat toil and slave, to human life save
These serving young men, young women so brave
Knowing life is so precious, they really do care
Rejoice brothers and sisters, in the world, everywhere.

bg2008

Yesterdays

Yesterday's distractions were fewer
Words and deeds, by far more pure
Overload IT vision on info highways
Few seek uncluttered, clear byways
Pollution in all pursuits now abounds
Yesterday's treats, nature's sights, sounds
Yesterday's values diminished to demise
Perhaps, ageing process is very wise
When a life has reached its purlieu
Yesterday's ways, too late to renew.

bg2011

Dare to Dream

Her looks not one for the books, not according to Hoyle,
Across the land a one night stand, this stodgy Susan Boyle.
A debut of triumph, success, cheering audience, defenceless,
With Susan it would seem, they too dreamed her dream.
Life changed beyond compare, her dream became the dare.
Critics and sceptics confounded, a soul piercing voice landed,
Moving, mellifluous to the ears, welling each eye with tears.

bg2009

Ode to a Gemini

As those who know you well can confidently attest
Your appetite is endless, for pleasure all that's best
Eager active life, feverishly lived right up to the hilt
With legendary Olympic stamina, rarely do you wilt
You have raised the benchmark, to such a heady height
Chagrin awaits lesser lights, though try as they might
Your motto may very well be: live love and be merry
Yet your wake is so littered; for some, it's all too scary.

bg2009

Prime Years Waning

His mirth and wit decline to sparkle
He turns and shuns life's debacle
Submits, resigns, to seek the sublime
Full well knows his enemy be time
If in quest for new love he should find
Dubious it will bring new peace of mind

His cup overflowing with health and grace
Not enough to win in a desperate race
Impartial almanac marked an onerous year
Real enemy, or phantoms beheld everywhere.

bg1980

From the Coalface

A mask of despair was etched on her face,
From what hill or height had she fallen from grace?
What was the price for this middle aged mother?
A lost spouse or for some reason or other,
Though common a sight as it may be,
Coalface reflecting, is still disturbing to see.

bg2008

Bradley Garrett

Transition

Youth has come, youth has left
It passed so quickly, was it theft?
All that strength and all that power
It blossomed and died like a flower
Not the least bit of help or use to know
That all men before me were dealt the same blow.

bg1981

Roadside Ballad

When suddenly life is cactus,
it may give rise to a curious practise.
Roadways littered with cross and flag,
fresh flowers too, another tag,
a loved one's reminder of a soul so dear—
a broken body once lay here.
Strangers, friends and visitors new,
know at once to be more careful too.
Speeding through culverts and curves
can be awfully bad for your nerves.
Each driver note and mark well this site,
where alas another's soul took flight,
lest in the light of another day,
you too may go the very same way.

bg2009

Bradley Garrett

What do you make of it?

Climate change is apparent now,
pestilence and famine follow the plough.
Rain here, no rain there,
we all will need to learn how to share.
Social fabric washed away in flood,
people and possessions consumed by mud.
The other hand is drought and dry,
families and farmers begin to cry.
with no food to share as loved ones die.
What do you make of it?

Now, as the ice shelves melt and the seas begin to rise,
Please, do not throw up your arms and act with surprise.
We've made fun of the 'greenies' and of all they pursue,
Tree huggers and do-gooders who thought that they knew.
Now the fight that they fought for has all come true
Now, it's we who feel blue. What do you make of it?

bg2008

A Very Good Year

Each sunny day is one to revere,
Have the eye shed not a tear,
Cast aside each and every fear,
The presence of plan is clear,
So work your plan my dear,
Keep your health and cheer,
To ensure your very good year.

bg2008

Classic Beauty

Your face.
Davina, my dear, my dear
Your face
caused many to cheer, to cheer
Your face
after yesteryear, after yesteryear
Your face
Still near to us; to us still dear, still dear
Your face
We see, still here, still here!

bg2012

Wheelchairs and Prams

Terrorist P plate drivers surround the town
Reverse peak cap, speeding, acting the clown
Invasive radio blaring, blasts the main street
Showering shops and cafe patrons as they eat
Obese pedestrians smoking with a can of coke
Appear amused, see the intrusions as some joke
Young girls with their babies in prams abound
Proudly parading, with a walk and look around
Active oldies in wheelchairs are there and about
Unable to walk, doggedly determined to be out.
In a town with no where to go and not much pay
The locals seem happy—don't want another way.

bg2012

Bradley Garrett

Early Morning – Bird Songs

When the night darkness begins to decay
The first hint of light at break of day
Wafting warbling bird songs begin to play
Firstly, familiar known tones we have heard
Surprise comes next from this adventurous bird
Follows, as twisted sounds of triffids and trills
These exotic echoes that strangle the quiet
Jangle awakening senses to shock, and thrills.
Morning calm and composure, allayed by disquiet.

bg2012

HARDSHIPS

'Now hear this'
Shape up or ship out
To pass the muster
Cut the mustard.
Shape up or ship out.

bg2012

Individuals

One's psyche afar removed, from populace opine
True to oneself, not owned by secular mankind
Spiritually ensconced in a grand Universe Divine
A Utopia of heavenly harmony, affixed in rock
In a pure rarefied zone—where eagles don't flock.

bg2012

Death's Door

My Brother, his dying demeanour devoid of demons;
Calibrated calmness, stemmed from certainty, uncertainty removed
A blinded bond between brothers, a lifetime to discover
Dormant love, life's lost treasure emerges to torment
Appears as a diamond exposed, sparkling in the day light dust
Enriching, stirring, unveiling the depths of heartfelt emotions.

bg2012

Afternoon Seabreeze, Gold Coast, Oz

Wind whipped sand stings body face and hand
Foamy friendly swells, offer respite on demand
After lunch sun provides an over browning tan
Equal opportunity for both woman and man
Swimmers outside flags hear a life guard berate
As a blaring loud hailer warns danger, their fate
Receding waves find gulls scouring the beach
Seeking elusive fleeting food, seldom in reach

bg2013

Moreton Bay—Sand Crabs—20th Century

In fifteen foot of water off the Cleveland point cutting
At all times the dillys gun place, for sand crab rutting
Female Jessies were found in about one haul in four
Granted freedom, to preserve the process evermore.

On occasion a visitor spurious is spotted near the hull
Moreton Bay excursions at sunrise punctuated, rarely dull
At just five feet, a young grey nurse foraging in the shallows
Passively hauled to the surface by these fishermen fellows
His cross saw teeth firmly fixed, clamped to the shinbone bait
Attached by string across the hoop, stolen via the open gate.

The sun is up, it's nearly seven, what's in the bag states breakeven
The shark arrived and made the point, pack up now and leaving
Outboard started and revving, haul up the anchor, and coil the rope
Enough excitement and adventure had, as much as we could cope.

bg2012
Dedicated to the late Syd Lloyd.

Sixties Nouveau

Night and day, day and night the 'bistro' was the new light
Mum, dad dragged in, to new eating order, no infradig in sight
Emboldened young folk challenged to embrace the change
Drinking dinner wine after starters and departing mid range
Single women early twenties blossoming beauty, milky white
Office party lunch by day, boyfriends and parents by night
Young, old, et al, discovered modern method eating serene
A decade on, the Bistro, a great Brisbane City meeting scene.

bg2012

Stress and Strain at the Pub

Shit a brick; Stone the crows;
The trouble I'm in; Nobody knows.
Struth, it's my shout!
Bloody hell!
Money has run out!
Shite has hit the fan
Likely cop a lengthy ban.

bg2012

Falling Apart

When if falling from a great height
Deleterious, any deliverance to save you
Nor favour or hand to help you, in sight
Make the journey with as little a 'to do'
Muster manners and grace bid fond adieu
What ever will be will be, 'C'est la vie'.

bg2013

Good Deed

It's no bull caffeine may give you a high
Or be uplifted clear like clouds in the sky
Kindness act inures joyful tear to the eye.

bg2013

Be Cause

If you love what you do
You may never a day work
Be goodness, love and happiness
Be who you really want to be
Wishing may leave you wanting.

bg2013

Twilight

If I am not here, then I am nowhere
Traveling the past is somewhere
My psyche often flies there
Seeing old friends at life's stages
Young and old through the ages
Some long dead are still grieved
Though smiling faces are retrieved.

bg2012

Hauteur

In vain he ventured to disguise haughtiness
Enacting an occasional venial naughtiness
Manners excel, above 'paragon of politeness'
Predatorial, caring little for opinion, others say
'We and they' mantra, where losers ought pay!
He worked harder at winning to make his day.

bg2013

Truculence

Pray Australia, nation of plenty, of fairness and patience
Becomes not a receptacle to harvest hearts of truculence
From far fields, where lay fallow, intolerance, turbulence.

bg2013

Forgiveness

Forgiveness: THE ALL THERE IS describes it so:
"Forgiveness is the fragrance shed from the violet
On the heel that has crushed it."

bg1980

Leg Up

Priority of a great nation: must be education
Penury voided by altruism, not robed vocation
Offspring, our children do not choose a parent
That are healthy wealthy wise, maybe aberrant
S'il vous plait! Forget not the child of this land
Grant every chance to live a life that is grand
This great country ushers many a gift, chances
Citizens who have much, enough—lift up your heart
Not by chance, ensure the future, give kids a start.

bg2013
Dedicated to the The Smith Family and the many like-minded organisations.

Life is Good

Many may not perceive a world that is perfection
While others live a life bathing in its reflection
Knowledge and experience the road to contentment
Followed by wisdom, the solving salve and expedient.

bg2012

Quandary

If 'Being' is the exponential arm of the Universe
One might ponder how "All Knowing" is converse:
To earthly challenges armed only with earthly wit,
One or more terms, facing Eternity at the end of it.

bg2013

Beware the Iceman

Iceman, come what may—no ice today.
Folk laugh—Folk cry—matter not you say
Life is good—Life is Feckless—or Fay
Be happy, be sad, for one more day.

bg2013

Utopia wanting

If life's journey has made you no enemies,
It follows, likely, you've made few friends
Panacea presence, no recorded testimonies
Look to the message bank the Universe sends.

bg2013

Ulmara

Circa 1860-Clarence River Port. NSW. Ulmara War memorial park: For God, King & Empire. A proud history of district Ulmara's 2,000 residents, yarns about men at arms:

1914, twenty-six men, Bailey to Waugh lost
                          in this first ghastly World War
1939, twelve men, a nursing sister, Anderson to Watkins,
                          thirteen more.
The town of just two short blocks, a pub, post,
                          a menage of fairytale shops
Features—Lily's Lair—Jack a Dandy, naming just two
                          that Willy Wonka sent
Time warp premises, Coldstream, Ulmara's main street,
                          'For Sale', or 'For Rent'.
On flat flood land, surrounding cane fields are spiked
                          by occasional dairy farms
Residents revering their kin, proudly tell yarns;
                          of heroic, stoic young men at arms.

bg2012

Esprit de Corps

Willy was wild for the last time, now it's just a glass of wine
Women are marvelous, really just fine, most, simply divine
Intelligence, gathered wit galore, should one want any more
Memories can tantalize, wily willed senses refuse to vitalise
Life's glass half empty or half full, many save half to fantasy.

bg2013

Golf: 'Sword of Damocles'
Paralysis by Analysis

Will I do this, or will I do that?
Is it this way or maybe that way?
Which is better, which is it best?
Brain paralysed, void and numb
Desolate feelings of struck dumb
Don't know finger from thumb
Many lessons too much thought
Sorting out as to what one ought.

bg2012

Love Thy Neighbour

The crook or crozier and fidelity ring
To poor, needy, does not mean a thing
Little relief in well versed parables
When one's stomach screams for edibles
Shame, countless corridors of administration
Accolade, payless workers, fight frustration
Like the Good Shepherd on hard knock street
Harvest humbled humans with naught to eat.

bg2013

(When this poem was written, I was distraught by the sheer numbers of disadvantaged IN THE WORLD, who had fallen outside of SOCIAL 'safety nets'.
We have now, Pope Francis 1st, a holy man, as a Cardinal, Prince of the church, who had divorced himself from the trappings of office; elected, solely to cook wash and iron, in humble lodgings-catch the bus to all destinations to help --particularly into the stressed areas, where underprivileged, struggled on a daily basis to survive.
Here indeed was the 'Good Shepherd', seeing, feeling the pains on the street of hard knocks. Amen.bg.)

What Works!

There is oft times a better way to improve your every single day
Age no factor at any junction, to try to improve your every function
Tried and true is all very well, to adopt change, only time can tell
Just leave the door open to explore, better new ways than before.
Step outside the square, broaden lean parameters, perchance to dare.

bg2012

Journey of Life

Reaving rawboned callow youth
Unbridled behaviour, unholy truth
Autoerotism seas from the start
Testing, vexing the bravest heart
There lays delirium of dichotomy
One discovers, finds who is one not
Navigated course to stop the rot
Become one's best, claim autonomy.

bg2012

Home

Retreat is the home where one rests the feet
To drop one's guard away from people you meet
Eager years of enthusiasm to get it just right
Gives added pleasure when you come home at night.

The harmony of nature is right there to behold
Nesting birds in the trees that live to grow old
Bees are so busy hopping from flower to flower
Then to complete the cycle down comes a shower.

The stirring of a breeze seems to rustle the trees
Then leaves waft down as gentle as you please
They land on the wet ground and lay there to rot
No longer hot, the flowers and shrubs perk up a lot.

Magpies and Kookaburras contesting the space
Draw the contest and retire with grace
Lizards that are frilled and lizards that are not
Roam the lawns and gardens and eat grubs a lot.

It's all so natural and relaxing to see
I can think of no other place I'd rather be
Barking dogs can sometimes dismantle the peace
The interruption is minor for soon it will cease.

bg1980

At Dusk

Shrill bird sounds penetrate the dusk, to pierce eardrums
Like a rapier's thrust,
Flocks of birds descend from flight, as they prepare to
Roost the night.
What ensues is an unholy fight, as each one jostles for the space
That's right.
The row-de-dow is heard each evening, leaving aching eardrums
sorely grieving.

bg2009

Betwixt & Between

In the journey through life that starts happy and bright
The roads appear so straight, no turns are in sight
The pitfalls and hollows, though there, are unseen
Blinded by youth's eagerness, there is only hope and a dream.

To live day and night right up to the hilt
No thoughts of the house that might need to be built
Pursuing pleasure and love and not have a care
Until time leaves you stranded, devil knows where.

Now how many times can love come and go?
Before it eats out your heart and becomes the foe
Like a man who has been running, whose panting and blowing
His thirst can't be quenched, yet his cup's overflowing.

bg1982

Colour of Autumn

Layered deep neath shrubs and trees
Compliments of a fresh Autumn breeze
Barrow loads of golden brown fallen leaves
Having surrendered before winter's freeze
Now naked branches look stoically stark
Disrobed, exposing crinkled knotty bark
No sounds of singing birds having fun
Resigned to the mean era of the sun

bg2012

"Fair Go" to "Have a Go"

When the troops came home in forty-five
All Aussie gratefully cheered—glad to be alive.
Joy, optimism flourished, for a fresh life
Freedom at last from war's tyranny and strife.

Freedom's southern beacon, the great continent
Shining afar on Europe's despair and discontent.
Many migrate, determined to have a go, and teach
A work ethic of long hours, 48 hours not in reach
No down time at the footy, or cricket or beach.

La Dolce Vita was their personal domain
Second nature for their culture to entertain
Milk bars, coffee shops opened in proliferation
Thanks, and thanks from a grateful nation.

bg2012

All There Is

One's mind is a thought, not an object—that's a no brainer.
The brain is an 'actuary' organ employed by the former
Now to add the heart to complete the person as a whole.
Which is heart, body, mind; enveloped by one Universal Soul.

bg2012

Bounce of the Ball

Taking calculated chances is all very well
But, at the end of the day no one can tell
Timing, timing can govern the win or the fall
Whimsical fortune can be the bounce of the ball.

bg2012

Boat People–1770

Australian Aboriginals were to boat arrival people, hostile.
Towards new settling white folk was resentment and revile
Now the turn of white folk, confronted by Asian and Muslim
The church for comfort may preach, offer a prayer or a hymn
Extoll Christian virtue, not to love your fellow man is a sin
Show love, compassion, monitor-reshape your comfort zone.
Just like 1770, adjust perspective, to this invasive new tone.

bg2012

Formal Wear at the 'Kaffe'

Blend in pitch-black night
With a driven snow, white
Formal attired Magpie sight.
Strutting purpose and poise
Alert ever, the slightest noise
Scours the take away floor
Assessing bounty is his chore
Shoo-ed away, shown the door
Feathered misanthrope variety
Too aggressive for human society

bg2012

Home Sweet Home—"Food on the Table"

Life ended in his eightieth year
With the usual funeral, usual tear
My, how many family did attend
My, how many children did extend
Testament to a good family man
Children's children, his greatest fan.

The eldest son stood up and spoke
Said good things about a good bloke
Then one line that stuck in my mind
To me a line of an extraordinary kind
"There was always food on the table"

bg2012

Gold Coast–Main Beach

Early surf sun and run, can be fun
All age runners exercise due care
Main Beach Parade, cars everywhere
Score side streets to Tedder Avenue lead
Tiled tall towers built for visitors' need
Shadowy shame saved by landscape divine
Palms, Pandanus, hedges below Norfolk Pine
Minding myriad of annuals, flowers sublime.

bg2013

Anathema for the Dreamer?

Young friends, take courage, do not falter:
Prepare and ready to feast on life's great altar.
There is only one course you must not shirk,
Rewards heaped upon those who choose to work.
Pursue endeavours that please, come what may,
Maybe this pursuit is not work, even for a day.
Irony, such a contradiction, yet true, it can exist,
'Aussie', 'Have a go', the determination to persist.
This wonderful ethos in abundance may be found
In our homeland—countless opportunities abound.

bg2011

Hunter Valley–Bird Watch

Ready made birdbaths all over the terrain, fresh water puddles left by the recent rain
Eager Cubans and Wrens charge in at a dash, vigorous wing flapping makes quite a splash
Waddling ducks with a clutch of new chicks, enter the pond to teach lessons and tricks
White turtledoves aground as they stop, to aid digestion, peck at grit for their crop
Black waterfowls, red beak, and white pants, have a peculiar gait and a look of askance
Enter a high-pitched searching sonar sound, the elusive source nowhere to be found
Echoes of Kendall's 'Bellbirds' to be sure, this greenish small bird with a voice so pure
Elegant black swans inhabit a larger lake, enough room to dodge the Pelican's wake
Food and space enough maintains the calm, peace and tranquility, the Hunter elixir balm.

bg2012

Elegiac Air Waves

Awake thinking about my 'Guardian Angel' thing
Hearing the sounds of black cockatoos on the wing.
Ahh here! Ahh here! What message do they bring?
A riveting, reverberating requiem that they sing.

bg2011

Pokolbin Village–Broke Road

Swaggering wag tails beg and badger for bread crumbs or snacks
Divert attention at lunch, when reading the paper, or trying to relax
Hope Estate across Broke Road, grand concerts make it well known
At other times, mobs of kangaroos graze and call it home
Seemingly oblivious, to visitor coaches and traffic that steam past
It is all very peaceful and lovely to see, and in complete contrast.

bg2012

Opportunity

Be aware few limitations exist in this great land,
Life has a grandness of awakenings, to open the door,
To grasp the nettle, to conquer, discover and explore.
Our Universe begs life to observe ever so much more.
For therein lies the wisdom and awareness for every day
Nature's beauty and love abound, see yourself in a better way.

bg2012

Maternal Light

Your passing has not dampened our love dear mother
Blessed with style and grace your presence like no other
When your favourite arias appear, churns memories to revere
Emotions unsullied over years, treasured, held for one so dear
Hidden, buried deep inside, suddenly surface, alight as tear.
Unbridled passion for family, life, music song and art
To your cherished grateful children you did impart.

bg2012

Act on cue

When you have things to do
Be on the ball
When the brain gives recall
Curse and swear
Finding what should be there
You did not forget
Ennui, your reward and regret.

bg2013

Rapscallion

There is a rat in the house
I am chasing shadows
There is a rat in the house
Every sound gets my attention.

All seems quiet before retiring
Lights off, mind still inquiring
A wily intruder pads a dark domain
To burgle and plunder without refrain.

bg2012

Over the Line

Perseverance, persistence, is the answer by golly
There will be a way, if just keep grinding away
When down for the count, penurious price of folly
Alacrity and humour, help keep the dogs at bay.

bg2012

Regent Theatre–Brisbane

Where gilded gold gargoyles upon plastered walls stare,
As patrons eat popcorn, while reclining in their chair.

bg2012

Liberté

Perestroika, Glasnost's dying embers, are 'Pussy Riot'
These brave young warrior girls, dare not to be quiet
No agenda for east or for west, just for a life that's best
When Kremlin's mighty hammer struck and stressed.

bg2012

A Spiritual Message

When your 'ready sign' is showing, the Master will be near.
Be sure in the Absolute knowing an Almighty truth is clear.
The Universe's source of healing, will allay your every fear.
And be the protective hand over all that you hold dear.

bg2008

Semper Fidelis

Others' faults in focus, clearly observed
May give rise to a condition, unnerved
Confronted in clarity in truth, fidelity
Self mirrored and aped the grim reality.

bg2013

Invitation to Lunch
(An Exercise in Aussie-speak)

The usual procedures apply, and as many have threatened to attend, it may be advisable to arrive early to avoid being forced to sit next to someone to whom you owe money, or who has witnessed you in some indiscretion you would rather not revisit, or even someone who talks too much or tells off colour jokes.

Reponse in CJ Dennis jargon:

Well spare me days and stone the blinkin' crows is this a lunch of sorts, cootes and coves mongrels and beaus bashin' ears eatin' drinkin' and rorts here's me thinkin' Tatts was curl the mows bli-me makes a bloke wanna blubber—those thoughts.

bg2006

Time

Well goodness gracious me,
How the weeks roll by,
my, the weeks roll by.
Old movies make me cry,
make me cry.
Each day it's hard to try,
hard to try.
It is time to die, time to die?
Observe the sky,
the blue, blue sky.
Watch the time fly by,
and meditate, my my.
How the weeks roll by, roll by.
Well goodness gracious me.

bg2008

Summer Landscapes in Oz

Summer landscape in Oz
Slashing summer growth; in humidity, rain
Engages and excites sensorial, as it is slain
Reduced fodder for bushfires, if they arrive
Lessons from blue planet, on how to survive.

bg2019

Heaven For Me

Enthralled by what I see:
Soft winds coaxing clouds away,
Wispy white against endless blue sky.
Treasured blue planet stands all alone,
Showered with every grace to make man home.

bg2020

Morning Malarkey

Summer; black cockatoos, with forest red tail
Bellow signature blurts, surveying, as they sail
Interjecting at black crows; 'parliament' meet
Arrk arrrk!! Closes meet, as 'to beat' the retreat.
Unresolved dispute, crow crap continues all day
'Black' day indeed, much mayhem - and no pay!
Interesting each year, to witness the clash
Autumn leaves signal end, for both parties to dash.
Six hour parliament dissolved, and crowing abate
'Stone the crows!' - next year, try not to be late!

bg2020

Bradley Garrett

Today Is the Only Day We Have

Life errors are like stepping stones
Even a mini stage in 'Game of Thrones'
Can't know warm unless know cold
March on, march on, be brave, be bold
How deep the ocean, how high the sky
Imagination constrained by the mind's eye
Walk a straight line, uphill can stop you
Surprise and delight, discover the view.

bg2019

Pavarotti Passing

Untimely death has claimed victory
Stage now bare of its giant talent
Cruel work of fate, such a mystery
Globally, all nations as one lament
Maybe Heaven could no longer wait
Pavarotti, of the tenors, flamboyant
Maybe welcoming, at Heaven's gate
Was a stage, death ever so poignant

bg2021

Bradley Garrett

Persuasion of Black

So what is it about cruel summer's end?
Black cockatoos arrive to cry and sing
Sad, doleful dirges pervade every bend
As murder of crows - 'aarrk' to the table bring

Magpies abound, in smart black and white
Noisy peewees, lesser lights on the green
Lacking in stature, likely heard not seen
Currawongs sleek, a commanding sight
With majestic agility, glide when in flight

Black bantam-size choughs cram and cluster
So tightly bunched, seemingly scour as one
At grassed gravel pits, their regular muster
Noisy mynah shriek signals eating is done
When black becomes grey, spells end of fun.

bg2016

Oxymoron

Planet earth: a continent of contradiction
Beauty and horror wed, bred unholy distraction
Warring *Homo sapiens*, with weapons and mace
Yet viewed from space, an Eden of colour and grace
Harbingers: Christ, Buddha, Allah, and the rest
Extolling love, struck a mordant chord at best.

bg2016

Signs in the Solar System

You, universe, unyielding of your awesome scope
Human understanding bowed by infinite scape
Mere 'kind' might presume: Heaven, here on Earth
God's hand, ringed by blue sea with golden girth.

bg2017

Just 'Being'

There is something grand about 'being'
Being able 'to get about', enjoy each day
Hot, hot summers; to the Gold Coast fleeing
Exhilaration of receiving first job's pay
Magic moments of first love's flutters
Every mindful of dress, looks, hairstyle
Puppy love might perpetrate stutters,
Later banished by fortitude and guile
All too soon, time alters 'the presence'
Karma-loka may invade inner space
Reflection accounts your very essence;
May meritorious moments save grace.

bg2019

'Orange Sky' Founder

John Wilkins, Mother Teresa - for Aussie homeless?
'Orange Sky' - blue skies of 105,000 beings, under duress
Vans converted to wash and dry laundry and shower facility
Validates the vanquished, restores and elevates ability
Many with the arse out of their trousers; some did lose
Regretfully, for many more, one can only muse.

bg2019

Full Moon, at Large

Luminary lunar night light
Torches sullen sky to bright
Masking my face and sight,
Piercing my eyes shut tight.
Bedroom window's open delight
Eternity's selection: tonight.

bg2020 for Helen

Bradley Garrett

Willy Wag Tail

I could see that he could see
He could see that I could see

Combing the eaves
For elusive larvae of the spider
Human's dwelling house,
Larder and provider.

bg2019

Rainbow's End

Fill up your senses with blue sky alight;
Far horizons, peppered by clouds so white
Infinity far too much for folks to ponder
Fairy tale enigma, this endless blue yonder
From cloud's closet, a rainbow did appear,
Arching down to earth as a heavenly spear

bg2019

Summer Madness

High summer's plethora of punishing heat waves
Ignites transient crickets' chorus of one-note raves
As the gum trees, like Anzacs, stand stoically erect
Australia's native unbowed, earns love and respect.
Ubiquitous magpie maudlin, mopes in the shade;
Quietly contemplates, probably planning a raid.
Other restive life seek shelter from a relentless foe
Late afternoon breeze's reprise is next get up and go

bg2019

Everything Matters, Yet Nothing Matters

We are who we are, we do what we do
We can raise the bar, choose to be 'who'
Dollars count: assist care for less fortunate,
Provide shelter, may place food on plate
World pressure on poor multitude mounts
Any personal time, care, effort, counts.

bg2019

Bradley Garrett

Mother Country England

Chelmsford, in ancient county Kent
Oldies' home, before Australia went
At ancient 'The Writtle on the Green',
Worn working water wheel still seen
River's current was its source of power
Used for grinding of grain into flour
Beautiful borough in a royal realm
Queen Elizabeth R II, still at the helm.

bg2019

Ace Tennis Pros

Focus out-guns wear and tear
Turn back on publicity glare
No ounce of luck anywhere
Gun players do not despair;
Work ethic and ability get there.

bg2019

Camp Road Sentient

Fallen branches plus bramble, been cast aside
Crafty kangaroos may hop, barely losing stride
Crossing Camp Road can be unfriendly, dubious
Death-dealing carnage, fate of carefree curious
While shrieking bush-birds may navigate freely;
Arborists sentient, created conditions ideally.

Dedicated to Lance, wine-maker at Capercaillie Lovedale
bg2019

Victory in the Vines

Craig Brown-Thomas, blessed with ready wit
Can teach and talk wryly, with a steady hand
Questions, concerns, easily erased - puts paid to it
About wine-making, our dear Craig is well-read!

bg 2019

St Catherine de Siena, 1347 - 1380

Prepubescent, ascending into a state euphoric
Catherine of Siena began life journey historic
Unschooled, under privileged, persona eclectic
Her mother's 25th child - gave birth to a mystic.

bg2019

Who Are You?

Best start with: who are you not?
The answer lies in a thorny mire
Life offers good, bad, or tommyrot
Monastic may be a heavenly choir;
Real world life, far removed scene
With ups, downs, in Heaven or Hell
Rise to the top or fail - for 'has been'
Have a go, have something to tell!

bg2019

Oakey Creek Road, Hunter Valley

Brave Brokenback Range confronts due west
Resident galah flocks venting, in noisy protest
Locals at peace applaud soothing, empty space
Wine world uncluttered, abounding with grace
Grape vines, unperturbed, ignore march of time
While weary, regimented olive trees toe the line.

bg2019

Ebb Tide: Life Going Out

    What was life all about?
    It seems much about mother;
    Love bond surpassed all other
    Flagstaff rock on which to lean
    Steady starlight, ever to be seen.

bg2019

Channel de Beyers

Bush bird songs seduce the harshness of silence
Heaven's harmony offers absolution and penance
And:
Bellbirds pelt pings, ringing with stinging abandon
Mortifying penance for visitors, selected at random
And:
Then, at the top of the rise, greets a sight for sore eyes:
Vast northerly landscape - both delight and surprise.

bg2019

Oz Ground Up

Smoke smears, smudges north through south
Barren brown earth, nought for critter's mouth
Unwelcome signs banish bird's sight and sound
Traumatized trees shed dried leaves to the ground
All manner of life, startled; now Mankind, in fright,
Left to deliberate Maker's power and might.

bg2019

Greta, Hunter Valley

Expansive rolling plains, so distant and wide
Touching mind and heart, like a silent bride
A Great Dividing Range, bulwark to the west
Throws out its challenges to bravest and best
Roused inner emotions rise to the fore
A singular blue planet, in a universe galore

bg2019

What's the Score? Imp to Limp

From *femme fatale* to feeble faineant!
Agility, litheness, long departed tenant
Journeyed a noble path to motherhood
Solace-seeking, like a pixie in the wood
Privacy to permeate pleasure of before
Stored memories, in suitcase by the door.

bg2019

Gift of Life

Four-year-old's captured attention span
On 'Discovery Road' in the 'Universe Plan'
Who sees each day as a trove of treasure;
Blue planet Earth, glory box of pleasure
Now pray for all the hapless, heavy hearts,
Jaded by setbacks of life's stops and starts.

bg2019

West Wind: Terrible Day to Be Out In

Tragic tree branches, thrashing frantically in fright
Lord oh Lordy, been blowing through the night!
Rasping rusty grass grudgingly stands fast
Dry upon dry, perennial penance, living to last
Beggared bees, blown from bathing in flowering,
Seek respite in lonely lee, hungry and cowering.

bg2019

Smell

'The essence of wine tasting'
Because the olfactory gland is located close to the temporal lobe
In which memories are stored -
Man appears better able to remember odours than most other impressions;
Vinelink Tours - Hunter Valley.

bg2019

Latitude 40 South

720 ft of steel, a mere speck
32 ft - Plimsoll line to flight deck
Roaring 40 seas, man and boot vie
Through trough, rollers 40 ft high
Seamen tremble in wake of power
Duty watch harnessed in salt shower.

bg2019

Electricians mate B. Garrett - R50327

As recalled; from 1956, aboard the light aircraft carrier HMAS Sydney, sailing from Sydney to Freemantle

To Obtain Wisdom, Observe More

Good Earth gives we mortals much to appreciate
Enough being never enough; still, we supplicate
Daily distractions cloud marvels each day brings
Smell the roses and listen as the lovebird sings
Sunrise, sunset, snapshot of mountains, sky above
Universe engulfs human spirit with rapture and love.

bg2019

Wistful Winter Mornin'

Naked torso's embrace of the warm winter sun
Sans sand, sound of surging surf's beach run
Notional wind bathes body's opened pores
Winter's peaceful present to chance outdoors.

bg2019

Life

Before you know it, it's come and gone
Make sure your persona light has shone
Ebullience balanced with steely stillness
On Earth's stage of gladness and sadness.

bg2018

Eternity

Hail to the Heavens, to the Lord of light
Who showers Earth with sunshine bright
Colour beacon solitary, in bleak universe
Bard's font of inspiration for heroic verse
Wanton wonderings for life after death
Aging beings consider their last breath.

bg2018

Stillness

Grace and space, cradled in a country retreat
Unhurried stillness, wisdom for eyes to greet
Home's quietude usurped by racket, din, noise;
Vouchsafe vicariously visits, restores poise.

bg2018

Puzzlement

Drinking in the sight of falling rain
God's given gift for parched terrain
Without, all life on Earth be doomed
And every lifeform forever entombed
Daily miracles for living, 'Heaven sent'
Man in denial, vehemently gives vent.

bg2018

Pacific Ocean Angst

With relentless, restive pounding
Ocean shore awash, resounding.
Concert of a soulless night choir,
Cheerless spirits from Hades noir
While dim portfolio of patio light
On standby, til day breaks bright.

bg2018

Other Side of Humdrum

Richard Rohr, his mellifluous tones do deliver
Nouveau, fresh vital views, like a raging river
Revealing; power of prayer chants hold sway
Blocking intrusive thoughts that won't go away

bg2017

Bradley Garrett

Nebuchadnezzar's Ashes Ascend

Same sex unions wed
Blokes share the same bed
Women in same light
Bleed, a monthly sight

bg2017

Oh Me, Oh My

If you don't laugh, you will cry
It's just one of those days
Nothing's right, hard as you try
Head in a cloud, mind in a haze
To the drawing board, start again
Deep breath: now, pick up your pen.

bg2017

Exit Winter, Enter Spring

The south-south-west, at its mumbling best
Blanket black clouds block light as shrouds
Soon, Heaven-sent devilish thunder skies vent
Hark, hear this ye all: as crashing hail stones fall.

bg2017

Equity

Noir hands, white face, my Equity wall clock
Unpretentious, magnificent, simple piece of art
Time-keepers Omega, Vacheron doth thy mock
One plus half-volt battery volts sets you apart
Devoid style, glamour, languishing upon a wall
Constant reminder, bankable, each and every day
Headstone monument to my greatest mate of all
Unfailing reliability, steadfast loyalty in every way.

bg2017

*Dedicated to Roy, deceased 2012 at 82 years, mates for 63 years -
never a harsh word!*

True Blue D'Arcy Doyle

Post WWII, D'Arcy Doyle prints were all the go
Australiana, for returning diggers, 'curl the moe'
Aussie-bred 'Western Walers' in nulla-nulla scenes
Aboriginal culture captured in ochre and creams
East, Dividing Range; juggernaut jacaranda bloom
Sheltering the sweltering billabong's wilting womb
'For keeps' kids, playing marble on the dirt street
Blinkered horse and cartman observe players elite
Who could not but ponder on painting *For Keeps*
Deafening stillness at peace, as grown man weeps.

bg2017

Moot Point

Bad luck often disturbs, leaves distressed
Highlights the many happy times blessed
To know warm, you've experienced cold
Today is the only day, you have to hold
Take a breather, find a quiet open space
Observe nature, marvel at universal grace.

bg2016

Energy and Light

$E = mc^2$ - Einstein equation beyond compare
What else is out there?
Broader questions sunk in a mire of oblivion,
   cloaking oblivion
Trite, trivial sum total of everyday existence
   eking out subsistence
Perchance a safety device for human being,
   shielded from seeing.

bg2016

Arlington Memorial in Step

1938: Joe Louis took Schmelling's title crown
Fight-fans gasped when the Nazi went down
American black man made the world aware
High-handed Hitler, found new ways to scare

Arlington Cemetery: America's most revered
Joe lies with 175 notables' remains interred
Vocational soldiers patrol 24/7
Evermore salute her heroes, home in Heaven.

bg2016

Bradley Garrett

Given the Opportunity

Were you born with a silver spoon,
Or was it more the slippery slide?
Former, chances you over the moon;
Conversely, have one helluva ride.
Verve, lethargy - love, hate - joy, strife:
A wondrous world, to have a life
Experiences are a vertical measure
Exhilaration, despair - life's treasure.

bg2016

Karma-Loka: Verses 114

Solitude, music at ease, lyrics to please
Like quietly-sliding, soft-swelling seas
Lulled into sublime four-four time
Effortlessly; lyrics roll, sync into rhyme
Who's to say? maybe very soul at play
Captured in the being, an Earth day.

bg2016

Top Knot - Crested Pigeon

Maybe oldest domesticated birds in history
Great war navigators for Napoleon, Caesar
Stay-at-home birds return for their leisure
Guided by sun, magnetic fields? Is mystery.

Same family as the charming divine dove
Etiquette precise, scrupulous, quisquilloso
Fussy, punctilious stay-at-home flock also
Though might perceived being cut above.

bg2016

New England

Gamboling the great Guyra high ground
Magnificent country views are all around
Up four thousand feet, atop in rarefy air
Human spirit compelled to stop and stare
Sky ever upward, outward in endless space
Infinity grandeur serves a spellbinding ace
Overwhelmed human, left cowering in awe
Fleeting relief from a world's grief and war.

bg2016

Bradley Garrett

1940s Bread and Dripping

Great Depression, leading to Second World War
Little food found its way through the door
Butter and spreads were scarce and unseen,
Fighting soldiers' support the reasons being.
Non-combatants contributed in many ways
Older men and women, left to work for pays

A few baked bread-loaves could still be found,
Bought for a few pennies from the 240 pound
For ever-hungry primary- and preschool boys
Going without food, plus now, everyday joys.
Innovation became the key for modest success:
Bonus in baking trays, left in their usual mess.

bg2016

Grim Companions at Reaper's Door

Hunger pain shared in Great Depression years
Now at brother's death bed, holding back tears
How fleetingly life-years vanished, surged by!
In Reaper's sight, an incredulous question asked
With a cheeky grin: 'What you driving now mate?'
Wondrous humour prevailed, overruling cry
Self-pity devoid, in his bright light all unmasked
Sobered siblings trembled, increased heart rate.

bg2016

Bradley Garrett

Passage of Time

Physical capabilities diminish,
Even begin to fail;
As muscle-toning starts to wane,
Strength turns to frail.
Accumulated wisdom abounds
In a fertile, active brain;
Gives rise to accounting deeds
Framed in a refrain.

bg2016

Sounds of Silence

Cushioned 'caw' of currawong,
Soft as velvet gloves
Short, intermittent, not long;
Same as symbolic doves.

bg2016

Breath of Life

In Yiddish, *'Yahweh'* means to inhale, exhale.
Life's first and last breath is the 'Holy Grail'
Time being, the very first to very last breath
'Yahweh' on lips at birth; again, last at death.
Neither skin colour, nor religious persuasion
Has any bearing on the outcome of occasion.

bg2016

Seniors' Lunch

'Punishingly crowded' best describes club lunch annuals
Once a year, sightings measure marks, period of aging
An unstoppable regression of human condition, staging
Remembering names, places not kept in the manuals.
Hail-fellow extinguished, with an unknowing glance
When pleasure of recall dashed by return look askance
Still, revisiting of times and places, rewards of recall
Yesterday's energy and laughter, when men stood tall.

bg2016

Midnight Unfolding

Body-piercing sounds, at midnight-still came
Abject expressions of anguish, excruciating pain
Open corridors of Hell, haunted howling of horror
Mortal combat of mongrel dogs; sound of terror.

bg2016

Senior Years

The bugger of everything wearing out
Fair dinkum, gets up old codger's snout
Every little part has a turn feeling tender
Like a human condition, account render

It could be a tooth; or even, maybe, a toe
Delicate areas, anywhere else located below
Maybe even feeling uncomfortable in bed
Humbug ongoing, maybe enough's been said.

bg2016
dedicated to Alan

The Petition

A steely, stoic quiet, like a blanket hung
Pervaded the chapel before prayers begun
Parishioners after mass, gathered to pray
Supplicate Father's favour; Judgement Day
Sorrowful mysteries, of intense Rosary cant
Imploring, remember hour of death, rant
'Please forgive us, give us our daily bread'
Was prayerfully petitioned, what was said.

bg2016

Paradigm Down Under Perusal:
Test Cricket

Winning with bat and ball, the object of the game
Zeal, whatever it takes, without demur or shame
Sportsmanship, mateship, great Aussie paradigm
Statement for youth: discipline, fall into line.

While test being played with vigour and intent,
A world in chaos: war, death, displacement, dissent
Down Under, we turn our backs, look the other way
From mind-bending terror, destruction, disarray
Aware, we know our very nature; be benevolence
Tempered by a very real threat: ongoing violence.

bg2016

The New Oligarch: 2015

Murdered! 'Shot dead in Moscow' is the headline
Opined, ordered by deacon of slithering house
Duplicitous deeds of tyro, democracy in decline
Boris Nemstov, opposition leader, man not a mouse
Publicly putting Putin down, belies a life retention
Against Ukraine separatists, his bone of contention
Scars from 20 million Nazi murders, bleeding
Unhealed, a bridge too far, democracy not heeding.

2017, Putin jails Navalny, opposition leader elect
Peace be with you, dear 'brother', trying to set people free
Intrepid opposition leaders, a short life can expect
Free-thinkers still gather throughout Russia; we see
Families fighting, elusive freedom, so many have died
After 100 years or more, from the Tsars finally free
Oligarchs, or Oligarchy now, people's mettle still mired.

bg2017

People Business: Dichotomy

Say: we are all part of the 'whole part' apart
It would follow then, camaraderie has a head start
Principles abandoned from the joy of 'just being'
Liberated senses awakened, delirious by 'just feeling'
Free reign to roam, explore, leaving discipline fleeing
Wonderment, the incredulous awe of an endless universe
Usurped by Earth umbra; the good, the ugly, the perverse.

bg2015

Pretender to Paradise

No before, no after; every day, a new beginning
No past or future; only now, now is all there is
Roll up roll up, come see, come hear the show
Listen, I will tell you all I learned, all I know

Be entertained, be informed, drink in the scenery
An extraordinary journey, each visit to winery
Landscaped destinations amid raw rural scenes
Perpendicular seduction for elders through teens

Relax, enjoy, feel the stillness steal your heart
Together with sights, sounds; each play a part
Beguiling moments, stealing souls to impound
Momentarily snatched to above mortal ground

Inverse, far removed from crowded 'struggle street'
Here in Hunter we pray, we hope we can meet, greet
Treasures entreaty; all of above beckons you forth
Break from bondage, escape through the north

bg2015

Food on the Table

City fringes, favoured where derelicts roam
Men, women, all; folk with no family, no home
Happy home, fond memories, in ashes far away
Some privileged few may cadge a place to stay
Weary shabby street dwellers, threadbare worn
Merciful charity, rescues with love that is warm
Pecking order prevails at temporary respites;
St Vinnies, Sallies, provide refuge of nights
Too, may be some, who once been down on luck
Turned life around, indebted, time to give back
Life good; if you are set of mind and body able,
Be sure your neighbour has food on his table.

bg2015

Bradley Garrett

Leonard Cohen's Hallelujah:
by the Choir from 'The Street of Hard Knocks'

Everyone who hears will be moved by the lyrics
Piercing peals penetrate a most obdurate heart
Ragged, broken street-dwellers to play the part
Jangling all audience nerves to heart hysterics
Reaped from city streets, coaxed onto the stage
Humanity's least, released from a homeless rage.

Onstage, irascible misfits masquerading as a choir
'Hard Knock Street' their shabby address and attire
Jonathon Welch cajoled, soothed these sorry beings
Became a foundation stone for new life beginnings
Navigating nerves through each solo performance
Levitating lowly souls above daily dire circumstances.

bg2015

Thought-Provoking

An epiphany: experience impacts the soul
Invasive new direction may take its toll
Awakened wonderings implode the mind
Gifted from the Universe, sure to be kind
Wisdom and awareness, new tools of trade
Vantage-viewing platform, in heaven made
From out of the wilderness, The Messenger
Enters terminal for the heavenly passenger
To comfort a bankrupt world, full of stress
Gracing all with love, comfort, tenderness.

bg2015

If Only

Ageing: a potpourri of thoughts and reflections
Invasive memory floods, resists all deflection
Chances missed; alternatives spring to mind
Degrading thoughts stew in a pot unkind.

Tremors of excitement torment young people
Life obstacle, path hurdle, high as a steeple
'If only I did this', 'If only I had not said it'
Perfection is grand, sure - elusive for halfwit.

Enriched by scores of years to savour, to ponder
A rollercoaster journey, full of awe and wonder
Universe, its great gift: life as a human being
On planet Earth, of wonderment, awe, for seeing.

bg2015

The Bumbler

How many times can you put your foot in it?
Countless, it seems, if your name is Max Sennet
Born 1880, a thousand years away from today
Harsh barren times, humour was hard to find
Slapstick comedy, panacea aspirin for the day
Enriching blanched humour of stateless mind.

bg2015

Bradley Garrett

Lucky

How do we choose time, place of birth?
Emissaries of 'The Light', beamed to Earth
Consider twenty-first century to millennium history
Why here and now? How to solve the mystery?
Astonishing new technology, *caravelle* ease
Dick Tracy's wrist phone now here to please
No longer the domain of the 'landed gentry'
Opportunity galore in the twenty-first century
The era of C. J. Dennis was back-breaking tough
When loads of hard work was not lucky enough
Inverse of that is true today; please don't fret
When the harder you work, the luckier you get.

bg2015

Sulphur Tablets, 1942

Flaccid and feeble, lungs labouring every breath
Sprightly, lively lad of six, on rocky road of death
Home-care means exhausted, doctor called to see
His luminary presence accompanied by hefty fee
A room of blanched faces, worried and distracted
Tearily awaiting doctor's verdict of exam enacted
Bad news, as pneumonia was terror of the time
Sulphur tablets were best that he could prescribe
Alexander Fleming's penicillin would be just fine,
Still awaiting authorities to approve and describe
A well of water needed to make the sulphur work,
Or was it Mother's warm hand on his wet forehead?
She would neither abandon, nor her duties shirk
Her caring presence close, keeping up good stead
Hours later, crisis passed, the sweat begins to dry
Mother smiled; with tears of joy, she began to cry.

bg2015

Bradley Garrett

Ingenuity and Human Endeavors

Suppression of expression,
treading on your dreams
Painter John Olsen views
outside the square, it seems

bg2015

EIIR

In this crowded world of wonderment: EIIR
What an energetic, enigmatic star you truly are!
Stoic stickler for correctness, yet humbly proud
Equally mindful with elite company or crowd
Neither from heinousness nor glory did you shirk
Subjects carbon copy, the ethics of hard work
We all pray, long may we keep you in our sight:
Shining template of all that is good and right.

bg2015

Prosaic Choices

What kind of surface, which road do we choose:
Steadfast, bland, loyal to a fault, or footloose?
Hail fellow well met, triumph in every avenue
Celebrated and revered in the family retinue
Honoured in death by children, foe, and friends
Passage problematic, the prosaic rarely ascends.

bg2015

Quid Pro Quo

You win, I win, this for that
Fitting form of any contract

Rex. 1215, Magna Carta projects
Basic justice for all his subjects

Biblical base, form of altruism
Genesis of Stalin's communism

Red Coats army put to the sword
USA and Irish independence roared

French Revolution, peasants' plight
Marseilles to march into sight

In Oz, how about a 'fair go, mate'?
Be a good bloke, it's not too late.

bg2015

1950's East Sydney: Sonnet

Beppi's downstairs restaurant, off William Street
Dining destination of epicurean, a popular retreat
Angelo de Marco's men's barbers, stylists for the fey
Five Italian migrants who had never heard the word 'gay'

Through side easement outback lies a dark laneway
Here, come 6pm, sly grog operators start their day
N.S.W. licensing laws force pubs to close at six
However, 'Cross critique' muse, maternal matrix
Posted lookouts - keep knit, should coppers arrive
To save bootleggers' skin, allow business to thrive

Coco-Cola's imposing sign, an Eiffel of neon light
Signals stamping-ground for creatures of the night
Turn west, a plethora of fine fashion and fancy food
Plus a tiny trickle of shops, offerings vulgar and crude.

bg2015

Pro Bono Bird Feeder

Galah's white cap atop pink shirt and mail
Silky suede grey coat covers collar to tail
All very eye-catching and bright to behold
Table manners, bravado all noisy and bold

Occasionally, a piercing screech of alarm
Momentarily disturbs galahs eating calm
Crested pigeons fidgeting nearby, less polite
Impatient diners, bent on picking a fight

Eastern Rosellas arrive in a blaze of colour
At peace, leave space enough for each other
Victualler verandah views, distance of calm
Provider's feeding platform: tonic, elixir, balm.

bg2015

Medal Moments

Special annual occasions, medals are worn
Theatre of war mementos, one's heart to adorn
'I like your badges,' quips a girly six-year-old
Confident, bolstered by stories she'd been told
ANZAC Day beer musters, akin to a rostered list
Echoes from departing stairways: 'Can I assist?'
Small, recurring moments of warmth and love
Melting men's hearts; visited rewards from above.

bg2015

Welfare, 1960:
How Times Have Changed

Brisbane, early 60's: money melt-down, times tough
Jobs lost, jobs hard to get, families in rough
As paid-off young navy man, angling for his first job
Joined a queue of ninety, just one winner for the mob.
Buoyed, braced by winning, eager to engage his brief
Sailing behind wheel of new Holden, a welcome relief
In this alacrity, elevated state of clear conscious mind
Chanced upon a healthy hitchhiker, eager lift to find
Young, married, dependent wife and baby to support
This was day of joy, atonement in his getting job, work.
Desperate for income, job's suitability not his to shirk
Hunter Bros Human Waste Removal, one hell of a rort.
How small my victory to sit aside this real man, a hero
No government agency to lean on, no help forthcoming, zero
No shame in shit removal, money for food on the table
To dine with grace and love, he did the best he was able.

bg2015

Bradley Garrett

Curtain Calls:
Winston Churchill

Lineage of the mighty Marlborough heroics
In office he baffled, bewildered critical stoics
Departing office, neither disgrace nor disdain
A champion for England all did he remain
History records state he was one of the great
When he was relegated back to family estate
Peace prevailed for more than twenty years
When Winston, with family, at theatre appears
Only as all seated, was their presence noted
Then one man stood, stared, and began to clap
Spontaneously, the entire audience rose and voted
His 'V' sign remained raised; now stood this venerable old chap.

bg2015

Golf Lessons:
Tell Someone Who Cares

Sheridans: pristine conditions at North Coast golf club
Helped to induce the tyro beginners out of the pub
Outlook promises; Sunshine Coast lived up to its name
Picture postcards in pro shop showed exactly the same
Fairway crows busily engaged, scanning a white golf ball,
Offering already-bewildered golfers yet another pitfall

Resident breezy-bright golf pro, engaged in jovial banter
Explaining teaching benefits, adding his name not 'Santa'
Further extolled value in loose change at the end of play
You can call your mum and explain away your golfing day
From out of the do's and don't's, this is the important bit
Because believe me, this is so true, 'cause no one else gives a shit.

bg2015 Dedicated to Michael

Ellen

Ellen, Ellen, what stories they be tellin'
You'll be right, aye, you are a grand sight
Mama and me will keep you safe at night
Don't be afraid of the dark, worried or fright.

bg2015 Dedicated to Bernadette

A Load of Rubbish

A winding, inquisitive road meanders past grape vines
A world removed, away from the district coal mines
Open green pastures, with the odd tree left for shade
Offer cattle hot-swelter relief, a shelter ready-made.

On a corner, a shopping trolley, ignominiously on its side
Depicting a slovenly society, lacking character and pride
Still on the tourist route, a tad further along, not too far
Lays a brightly-coloured rubbish bag, thrown out from a car.

This beautiful, rural, clean, open, pristine country space
Despoiled by a handful of folk; misdirected human race.

bg2015

Bradley Garrett

AD: 1941

Depression and war were camped at the door
A five-year-old picked up crumbs from the floor
Eureka, older brothers discovered a grease 'drip tray
Treasure for bread crusts - first meal of the day!

White Russian migrants numbered but a few
Abandoned homeland for values held true
Most of our Aussie men had gone away to war
Uncertain times changed our lives evermore.

bg2020

H. V. Divine Cradle

Hills, plains, and valleys all, in an uncluttered space
Surely Universe's gift divine, from a heavenly place
Indeed, escape divine from city's traffic profusion
Welcome tonic, relief departing crowd confusion
Hear a concerto of bird calls, laying claim to each site
Echoing pleasantly through the day and into the night
See tiny rabbits appear, instantly bounce out of sight
What comfort do burrows offer? A cold winter's plight
Prolific number of galahs seen feeding on open ground
Nervously, cautiously peck, check, swivel head around.

bg2020

Contemplative

Pray you may find such a place to rest!
Universe afforded peace, I can attest
Uncluttered space, away from busy life
Elevates mind to clear, 'as sharp as a knife'
Julian of Norwich, God-given spirituality
Dualistic, duelling mind for any eventuality

bg2020

Heaven For Me

Enthralled by what I see:
Soft winds, coaxing clouds, go by
Wispy white against endless blue sky
Treasured blue planet stands all alone
With every grace, gives all life a home.

bg2020

Be Careful What You Wish For

Movie actor Robin Williams, USA Academy star
Serious, delirious, angry, sad - no character too far
A raft of roles he played, made one laugh and cry
Singular talent, beacon of light, chose death and die
Genius was the nemesis that deranged, derided his life
Really mundane, in a make-believe world, sans strife!

bg2020

Ghoulish Galahs

Groundless shrieking by ghoulish galahs
Clamouring, shoving to feed-dish forefront
Finally, a foothold to elusive meal, hurrahs!
Victory at whatever cost - no mean stunt.
Endless squabbling ensues, until plate empty
Lesson for tomorrow: be early, don't be late
Aussie male antics deemed noisy, out loud
Using the vernacular: 'galahs in the crowd'.

bg2021

Sign of Summer

Hello! a soft and silvery moonbeam
First of summer's high heaven-sent
My naked arm, awash with its gleam
Comfortable lodging, free from rent.

bg2020

2000 AD

His cross, awash with blood, sweat and tears
Crowned by thorns, Christ tormented to death
How much has life altered after 2,000 years?
Wages of sin, burden til the very last breath
Garden of Eden, could it be this planet blue?
It has all the hallmarks - stop, look and listen!
Sights, sounds and every kind of colour hue
Let the stillness being envelope soul to glisten!

bg2000

Bradley Garrett

My Squat

Walls of stillness surround my squat
Wildlife too seemingly like this spot
Oblivious to all traffic of humankind,
Save the clear thought in one's mind.

bg2020

Tranquillity

Be constant companion, the sound of silence
Stillness where open plains occupy the space
Open as sky above, moving wind to reverence
Mindful of what you wish, herein is God's grace.

bg2020

Cradle of the Universe

Hills, plains, and valleys all, in an uncluttered space
Surely 'Universe's gift Divine, from a heavenly place
Indeed, 'Escape Divine' from, city's traffic profusion
Welcome tonic relief, departing 'crowded confusion'
Hear a concerto of bird calls, laying claim to each site
Echoing pleasantly through the day and into the night
See tiny rabbits appear, instantly, bounce out of sight
What comfort do burrows offer, a cold winter's plight?
Prolific number of Galahs seen feeding on open ground
Nervously, cautiously peck, check, swivel head around

bg2020

A Stormy Night One Summer

A Lightning flash x rays the trees, and lights the night, before it flees.
Like a scene from a Hansen Gretel tale, Heavens rant and Heavens rail
Crickets creaking tones afar do fly, to be in concert with those nearby
Loudly proclaim their presence, cloaking night noir, with an eerie essence
Then hail and tempest of the summer storm, add cool comfort to the warm
From a firmament in high heaven sent, soon its fearful ferocity spent.
Then follows a defiant stillness, rest, at the departing intruder's behest.
Deafening silence in complete contrast, inverse equal to what has passed
Senses paralysed in the electrified space, soon return with normal grace
Gradually, movement in the night, breaks the spell of storm cast smite.
Vaulted in the sky, dwells a Talisman, universally playing out His plan
Signs off on this portfolio feature, for the good of man and every creature
Though power is cut, there is no light, peace may be found on such a night
May the tempest night pervade lands heart, rejuvenate a grand new start.

bg2009-12

Roving Rogues on the Wing

Plucky pukeckas chanced upon gratis grain
While carefully culling their adopted terrain
Resigned, the old man sat down on the grass
Sharp stone underlay, biting him on his arse
Resigned to agreeable outcome for this deal
As Galahs enmasse, arrived for regular meal.

bg2021

Gift of Universe

'Gift of Universe', seasons to wonder -
Way beyond a fiery ball in an endless sky
Unanswered questions abound till we die
A warm winter sunlight pierced a bed space
Caringly caressed a pillow's cold open face
Blue planet Earth, gem of known Universe
Garden of Eden laden with treasure diverse.

bg2021

Sounds of Summer

Soothing sounds of light falling rain
Perhaps a message from our Makers hand
Sent with love for all life on earth to retain
To placate mankind and renew the land.
All the while angry dark clouds complain
As if to grudgingly object to man's gain.

bg2022

"Whatever Works"
bg2022

To Fr. John Nee   85c(07) 3349 1558

Re Jesse May GARRETT (Joy)
born 13/05/1909.

Resided at Lenoroa since 1986.
Children (4) Des (73) Trevor (70) Bradley (65) Melodie (54) flown in from USA Wednesday 16th for a wee today.

Early memory during the war (1939-1945) she played piano in Queen St Store selling records & sheet music. On Sunday evenings after listening to the scary episode of "The Shadow" the whole family would have a sing a long around the piano — all participants with great gusto until exhausted — then off to bed —

She was a very handsome woman, not given to excesses. — She never drank alcohol or smoked cigarettes — Enjoyed robust good health.

When her family had grown up she studied and obtained a degree in psychology.

She had a number of positions in management and was personnel mgr for Myers Coopers. and Tritton Furniture City.

She always had a great thirst for knowledge — particularly the "ABSOLUTE" of the Universe and worked strenuously towards a better understanding of the relationship of - self - and the "ALL THERE IS" the ALPHA & OMEGA. —

SHE WAS TERRIFIED OF STORMS & OF DYING — IN THE PAST TEN YEARS HER CONDITION (ALZHEIMERS) RENDERED HER INSENSITIVE TO SUCH OCCURRENCES — SHE IS BEST REMEMBERED AS A LIFELONG (12)3126 CARING. FIGURE — A WOMAN OF GREAT SENSITIVITY — HER EXAMPLE OF MODERATION IN ALL THINGS AND HER COURAGE IN ADVERSITY.
BRADLEY GARRETT

Re: Jesse May Garrett (Joy)
Born: 13th May, 1909.
Resided at Canosoa since 1986
Children:
Des (73), Trevor (70), Bradley (65), Melodie (50). Flown in from USA for service.

Early ememory during the war (1939 – 1945): she played piano in our Queen Street Stores, selling records and sheet music.

On Sunday evenings after listening to the seary episode of "The Shadow", the whole family would have a sing a long around the piano – all participants with great agusto, until exhausted – then to bed.

She was a very handsome woman, not given to excesses. She never drank alcohol or smoked cigarettes. She enjoyed robust good health.

When her family had grown up, she studied and obtained a degree in psychology.

She had a number of positions in management and was personnel manager for Myers Coorparoo and Tritton Furniture City.

She always had a great thirst for knowledge, particularly the "ABSOLUTE" of the universe and worked strenuously towards a better understanding of the relationship of self, and the "ALL THERE IS". The ALPHA & OMEGA.

She was terrified of storms and of dying. In the past ten years her condition (Alzheimer's) rendered her insensitive to such occurrences.

She is best remembered as a lifelong size 12 figure, a caring woman of great sensitivity. Her example of moderation in all things and her courage in adversity.

Bradley Garrett

Acknowledgments

Thanks to Dr Allan Morse, Senior Lecturer in Visual Communication and Course Coordinator Visual Communication (Graphic Design) at the University of Newcastle. When we needed to find an illustrator, Allan put the call out.

Thanks to Fiona Tsang, for the illustrations that captured the tone of the collection with insight and precision.

Thanks also to Michael Jameson, for his editing and to Graham Davidson for his typesetting and layout, and for managing the project with patience and enthusiasm.

I would also like to thank Mr. Richard Mercer, my one time Golf Professional, for introducing me to such colourful, wonderful expressions. Thank you Adrian Symons, for writing such playful imputations of josh and banter in your 'invitation to lunch', which in turn prompted my rejoinder.

And thank you to my family and friends; to all persons, either known to me or unknown; to every creature; for every event affecting my life, seen and unseen; to each and all for being a part of the Earth's rich tapestry of life.

I share this with you.

Life is Good - bg

A Journeyman's Tales

www.ingramcontent.com/pod-product-compliance
Lightning Source LLC
Chambersburg PA
CBHW011801090426
42811CB00008B/1012